Me...
Valle... ....
Tonbridge ~ Maidstone ~ Rochester

Kent
WELCOME TO THE GARDEN OF ENGLAND

Designed and produced by The Design Studio and
Countryside Group, Kent County Council.

Authors -
Kev Reynolds
Annie Hood
Harold Eagles
Kent Trust for Nature Conservation

Illustrator - Sandra Fernandez

Photographer - Kev Reynolds (except where indicated)

Editor - Eila Lawton

Maps produced by The Design Studio with the sanction
of the Controller of HM Stationery Office - Crown
Copyright reserved

Printed in Great Britain by County Print

Published by Kent County Council, Planning
Department, Springfield, Maidstone, Kent ME14 2LX.

First published September 1996.

ISBN 1 873010 52 4

Medway Valley - Contents

Guidebook

Medway Valley

Medway Valley - Walk planning and preparation

Medway Valley - A story of its people and places

Medway Valley - Exploring the area

Further information and references

River Medway

The River Medway rises in the Ashdown Forest as a spring issuing from the Tunbridge Wells Sands just above Turners Hill in Sussex. The sands and clays of the High Weald (Hastings Beds) dictate the character of the river, which, with its many deeply incised tributaries, contrasts sharply with the chalk streams found in other parts of the region. The Wealden clays are impermeable to rainfall and water must find its way across the surface of the steeply sloping land, creating a multitude of small rushing streams.

These meet to form a typical Wealden vale as the Medway flows north-eastwards towards Penshurst. There, the river is joined by the River Eden. As it flows across the Vale of Kent the gradient is less, though the river still collects tributaries which rise in other parts of the High Weald. These include the Rivers Bourne, Teise and Beult. The River Teise has mixed origins; the Upper Teise once flowed eastwards to the Rother but was captured by the Lower Teise when it cut away the soft clay ridge dividing the two streams. The River Beult which rises in the Greensand ridge is the longest tributary of the Medway. The scenery along this section is typical of a wide flood-plain.

The Medway cuts its way through the Greensand ridge beyond Yalding and collects two more tributaries, the Loose Stream and the River Len, before reaching the county town of Maidstone. The Loose Stream for part of its length flows underground. The River Len is larger and longer, but flows more slowly and has its source near the village of Lenham. Unlike the tributaries arising in the High Weald, the Loose and Len have more reliable springs which sustain their flow through the summer months.

Allington Lock forms the tidal limit of the Medway in Maidstone, a reach of some $12^1/_2$ miles (20 km), from whence the river flows north, cutting through the chalk to create the Medway gap.

Here the land rises more than 440 feet (135m) to the east and some 590 feet (180m) to the west. At Burham, looking towards the chalk scarp, the Medway gap gives the finest impression of the enormous amount of eroded material that must have been carried away over thousands

Otteshaw, Hartlake (Medway River Project (MRP))

of years. It is perhaps difficult to imagine that the chalk covered the Wealden dome some 80 million years ago and has gradually been weathered and eroded away. Rivers that once radiated out from this dome have assisted in the erosion process, carving their way through both hard and soft rocks to create the typical ridge and vale landscape we see in the Medway catchment area today.

The river widens between Rochester and Sheerness until it flows into the Thames Estuary and, from there, the North Sea.

The total length of the Medway proper from source to the estuary at Sheerness is 70 miles (110 km).

As the river gradually loses height on its route towards the sea, a series of locks and weirs were created as part of the Medway Navigation. From the 17th century, river traffic carrying a variety of raw materials was able to travel some distance up and downstream. Today, however, most river traffic is confined to recreational use.

Water Quality

The Environment Agency sets objectives for river quality to protect natural stocks of fish and the uses to which the water is put. To achieve these objectives, the authority sets limits on all permitted discharges to the river, restricting their strength and quantity. These are known as consent conditions.

Historically, urban development and industrialisation have taxed the river's ability to absorb waste. However, the Environment Agency and its predecessors have been able to bring about improvements by imposing increasingly more stringent consent conditions.

Low summer flows and high temperatures make Wealden rivers less easy to protect than the chalk streams in other parts of the region. The risk of pollution from agricultural activity is a significant factor,

Tonbridge meadows (MRP)

especially in the High Weald where there are many small dairy farms. The steeply sloping land and the impermeable clay aggravate the effects of slurry and silage pollutions, particularly during periods of heavy rainfall.

Between Tonbridge and Maidstone the river flows through the 'Garden of England' where fruit growing predominates, sometimes giving rise to pollution from agricultural chemicals.

Population growth in Tonbridge, Tunbridge Wells and other commuter areas has resulted in greater quantities of treated domestic effluent being discharged to the river. In particular there are relatively large sewage treatment works on the River Eden, the River Grom, the Somerhill Stream and the Botany Stream.

Historically, the naval base at Chatham gave great economic impetus to the lower reaches of the river and its estuary. Urban and industrial development have been significant factors affecting the water quality. The principal discharges comprise effluent from the

Angler on the Medway

tench. Minnows, gudgeon, stone loaches, bull-heads, brook lampreys and perch are also found in riffles.

The main river has considerable angling interest over its entire length and attracts large numbers of fishermen. The upper reaches support chub, roach and pike along with several other species. The stretch below Ashurst Weir has a breeding population of barbel and is an important spawning ground. Grayling have been stocked to the upper reaches over recent years and some also find their way down the River Teise into the River Medway.

Eels are not so prolific in the Medway catchment as on the Kentish Stour and the River Rother. In wet years the occasional sea trout or salmon is reported but existing water conditions in the estuary prevent a self-sustaining population from being re-established at present.

paper and chemical industries, cooling waters from power stations and sewage effluent from several large treatment plants. Apart from the cooling waters, all effluent is treated before discharge to the estuary.

Motney Hill and Aylesford Sewage Treatment Works are the two largest in Southern Region.

Under normal flow conditions, effluent is diluted and dispersed in the tidal waters of the estuary. However, at times of low flow and high temperatures the upper reaches can become substantially devoid of oxygen. This is aggravated because the major polluting loads are imposed towards the head of the estuary. To meet the challenge, the Environment Agency plans to review consent conditions on discharges to improve water quality in the estuary.

Fisheries

The iron-rich streams of the Weald support resident populations of small but highly coloured brown trout. The River Teise is managed as a game fishery down to Marden whereas the lower stretches of both the Teise and Beult are managed as coarse fisheries with chub, dace, roach and pike. In the middle and lower reaches of streams where the water is deeper, there are bream and

Geology

Between Tonbridge and Rochester the River Medway flows through three main geological areas: Low Weald, Lower Greensand and North Downs.

Low Weald

Rose bay willowherb

This low-lying and broad clay vale merges gradually and gently with the High Weald to the south and more abruptly and dramatically with the Greensand to the north, especially in the west of the county. Weald clay covers almost the whole area, its wetness and heaviness, combined with the generally flat, low elevation, causing natural drainage to be poor. The clay is not uniform, varying from very acidic to calcareous and a consequently richer flora. The soils in the west are more or less a heavy loam and suitable for cultivation.

The soils in the valleys of the Medway, Beult and Teise to the east of Tonbridge have given rise to orchards and hop gardens interspersed with small fields of arable and pasture and occasional blocks of woodland, creating a diverse and changing landscape. Riparian vegetation tends to be stronger than elsewhere, with ponds being of considerable ecological importance, whilst hedgerows are less prevalent, particularly amongst the orchard areas. Loss of orchards and creation of larger arable fields would dramatically alter and impoverish this area.

Lower Greensand

This belt of countryside forms a distinct scarp and dip slope topography throughout much of its length, although it is quite different in character to the chalk landform to the north. There are four geological formations within the Lower Greensand - Folkestone Beds, Sandgate Beds, Hythe Beds and Atherfield Clay - and, in landscape terms, the thin belt of Gault Clay immediately to the north forms a part of this zone. Folkestone sand is coarse-grained, acidic and

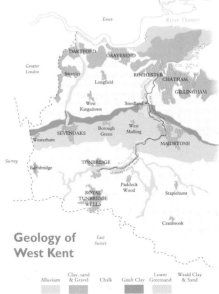

Geology of West Kent

Alluvium	Clay, sand & Gravel	Chalk	Gault Clay	Lower Greensand	Weald Clay & Sand

very free-draining, resulting in a number of heaths and commons, especially to the west. These are often of high value for nature conservation. Sandgate Beds are heavier and wetter, with the result, in past times, of a good deal of pasture. Hythe Beds, which form the escarpment itself, consist of a calcareous sandstone or ragstone and give rise to a rather heavy loam of wider agricultural use. This soil also supports woodland areas of national importance for nature conservation, and occasional unimproved grasslands with the calcicole, or lime tolerant, species creating a contrast with the acidic Folkestone Beds. Atherfield Clay is a stiff blue clay below the Hythe Beds that forms a thin

outcrop at the bottom of the scarp and merges with the adjacent Weald Clay.

From the Surrey boundary in the west to Pluckley in the east, the scarp face of the Lower Greensand Hythe Beds is a marked feature, increasing in height westwards to a maximum of 800 feet (245m) at Toys Hill. The dip slope reduces gradually in elevation towards the north. The linear valley created by the dip slope and the North Downs scarp, and including the intervening belt of Gault Clay to the north, is often called the 'Vale of Holmesdale' and runs broadly west to east through much of the county.

Fruit and hops are dominant features on the fertile soils of

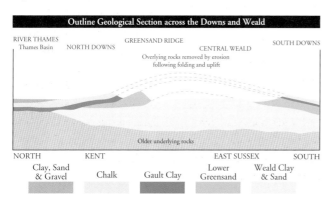

the lower dip slope centred on the Medway Valley and extending from Mereworth in the west to Kingswood in the east.

It remains an area of many orchards separated by poplar or alder windbreaks, small arable fields often in horticultural crops, all punctuated by quite regular blocks of woodland, much of which is chestnut coppice, and occasional hedgerows. Certain parts of the Medway Valley are very vulnerable to conversion from orchards to arable, a process which has already commenced.

North Downs

To the north of the Gault Clay, the North Downs scarp

rises abruptly above the Vale of Holmesdale and descends far more gradually towards the Thames Estuary and the North Sea.

These northern chalk downs extend from Farnham in western Surrey to the Kent coast at Dover. In Surrey, most of this downland lies within the Surrey Hills Area of Outstanding Natural Beauty (AONB). In Kent it forms the Kent Downs AONB and covers 316 square miles (845 square km) of some of the most beautiful and hidden countryside in the county.

The designation of the AONB was confirmed in 1968, giving formal

Outline Geological Section across the Downs and Weald

RIVER THAMES
Thames Basin NORTH DOWNS

GREENSAND RIDGE

CENTRAL WEALD

SOUTH DOWNS

Overlying rocks removed by erosion following folding and uplift

Older underlying rocks

NORTH	KENT		EAST SUSSEX	SOUTH
Clay, Sand & Gravel	Chalk	Gault Clay	Lower Greensand	Weald Clay & Sand

recognition to the natural beauty of the landscape. It is particularly valued for the dramatic south-facing scarp, the secluded dry valleys, the network of tiny lanes and its isolated farms and churches. It is an area of ancient woodlands and traditional unimproved grasslands, scattered oast-houses and small orchards, and includes the dramatic white cliffs at Dover. Parts of the Greensand ridge and of Romney Marsh are also included within the designation.

Unlike the Greensand ridge the chalk scarp is distinct throughout the length of Kent, although it too is generally higher in the west

than in the east. The dip slope itself is generally broader west of the Medway and east of the Stour than it is in the centre. It gradually reduces in height in a northerly direction away from the scarp.

Extensive woodland cover is present throughout the North Downs, both on the scarp face and on the upper dip slope. Scarp woodlands serve to emphasise the prominence of the landform as well as being a unique feature in their own right. Until recently the land use was predominantly pasture, but there has been increasing arable cultivation which has posed a considerable threat to both tree cover and unimproved grassland. Elsewhere, the decline of grazing on steeper slopes, especially by sheep, has resulted in considerable invasion by shrubby chalkland species. These trends increasingly threaten the unique landscape and wildlife value of open chalk grassland on the scarp face.

The Medway Valley, running between Maidstone and Rochester, divides the Kent Downs AONB into two sections. In common with the other river valleys crossing the downs, this was one of the earliest areas of permanent settlement in Kent. The long history of human activity in this area is illustrated by the group of pre-historic sites, such as Kit's Coty standing stones, which form the most important group of megalithic monuments east of the Berkshire Downs. There are several Roman sites here and the ancient trackway now known as the Pilgrim's Way passes through this area.

The AONB covers the scarp and scarp-foot within the Medway Valley, but excludes the industrial valley bottom. Despite the urban

Medway Valley

An Area of Outstanding Natural Beauty

developments, however, the Medway Valley provides an important rural buffer between the sprawling conurbation of the Medway towns and Maidstone.

In the north, a small area of flat, riverside marshes is included within the AONB. Although dominated by overhead wires and pylons, the narrow, scrub-flecked ditches and rough tussocky grass give the area a slightly incongruous sense of wildness.

Natural History

The Medway valley contains some significantly important stretches of wetland habitat interspersed with large areas of intensive agriculture and urban land. Wetlands are increasingly under threat from industry, drainage, water abstraction and other development. To help conserve remaining wetland habitats along the Medway valley, areas have been designated as Sites of Special Scientific Interest (SSSI) because of their national wildlife importance. Some other stretches have been designated as Sites of Nature Conservation Interest (SNCI) by the Kent Trust for Nature Conservation.

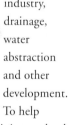

Frog

Tonbridge

Downstream from the Great Bridge an old brick revetment has a fascinating collection of plants typically associated with walls, including hart's tongue fern, pellitory of the wall and ivy-leaved toadflax.

Where vegetation is established in the urban area, willow and alder grow in the damp riverside soils. The seeds of the alder provide a winter food source for birds, including visiting siskins and redpolls.

A wide variety of riverside plants can be found along stretches of the river, including the colourful purple loosestrife, orange balsam, comfrey, gipsywort and water forget-me-not. One particularly invasive and alien plant growing here is the Himalayan balsam. Without control this plant rapidly chokes the less vigorous plants, reducing the variety and subsequently the wildlife interest.

Below Cannon Bridge large anthills can be seen in the wet meadows. These are an indication that the land has not been disturbed for a very long time. The anthills frequently attract the green woodpecker in search of a tasty meal.

East Peckham

Towards East Peckham and beyond, the path passes by a series of small woods and copses with a number of dykes crossing the arable land. Sections of this stretch of river are designated SNCI. Common oak, ash and hazel grow on the drier soils with alder and willow in the damper areas. Wildflowers include bluebell, moschatel and ramsons or wild garlic. Two uncommon plants found here are the narrow-leaved

bittercress and the greater chickweed. Amongst the woodland plants are a number of lichens and mosses including some species specific to the Medway.

Many birds feed and nest in the trees, shrubs and reeds along this section of river, including the nightingale and several species of warbler. The dykes attract dragonflies and damselflies including the southern hawker, common darter and banded damoiselle. In summer look for emerging adults on the stems of waterside plants.

Yalding

Adjacent to the river at Twyford Bridge is Yalding Lees, an area of agriculturally unimproved grassland. Despite heavy visitor use many wildflowers grow here, including bird's-foot-trefoil, lady's bedstraw, burnet saxifrage and tufted vetch. In turn these plants attract bees, butterflies and other insects. At the western edge of the Lees a line of old crack willows is a likely spot for roosting bats and owls.

Nettlestead

Upstream from Nettlestead the path passes Waregraves Wood. The wood lies on a ragstone slope and is largely of ash coppice with oak standards. The damper areas nearer the river are dominated by alder and willow. A calcareous stream runs in a small gill towards the river. Plants growing here include bluebell, yellow archangel and dog's mercury, an indication that the wood is likely to be a remnant of ancient woodland. Ferns flourish in the damper areas, including broad buckler fern and male fern, with golden saxifrage and water figwort growing by the stream. Woodland birds here include the wren, great tit and nuthatch. Passers-by may also be lucky enough to hear the characteristic 'yaffle' of the green woodpecker.

Teston

At Teston Bridge there is an array of riverside vegetation including comfrey, hemp agrimony and purple loosestrife. In the river itself

Medway below Maidstone

the emergent yellow water lily and arrowhead can be seen. In spring common tern may be seen performing their spectacular aerobatic diving display. There is also the chance along this and many other stretches of the river of catching a glimpse of the iridescent blue of the kingfisher. Adjacent to the river here is the Kent County Council Picnic Site. This open grassland has a wealth of wildflowers in summer, including bird's-foot-trefoil, meadow vetchling and creeping buttercup. Visitors should be aware of the presence of giant hogweed, a plant that can cause blistering if touched, and the highly dangerous hemlock.

In summer the grassland and surrounding shrubs are filled with sight and sounds of bees, butterflies and other insects. In spring the marshy area close to the river is a mass of frogs using the pools of water for spawning, a now unfamiliar sight in rural areas. Kestrel may be seen hovering over the rough grassland in search of voles.

Maidstone

Between Barming and East Farleigh Bridges, a number of small streams flow across the rough grassland. One unusual plant found here is the giant horsetail.

On the outskirts of Maidstone town centre there is a mix of grassland with some woodland. Horse chestnut and sycamore are two alien species found here; these non-native trees are of much less wildlife value than most of our native tree species.

Below Allington Lock the river is tidal and the mudflats exposed at low tide are visited by birds such as mallard and redshank.

Aylesford

North of Aylesford the path passes through the Holborough and Burham Marshes SSSI which includes the Kent Trust's Burham Marsh Nature Reserve. Here there are extensive reedbeds together with wet meadows, open water, scrub and

woodland. The reed beds are dominated by common reed and are home to the reed warbler, water rail and occasionally the rare bearded tit. In the wet grasslands lapwing and redshank regularly breed. An unusual plant found here is the marsh mallow, larval foodplant of the nationally rare marsh mallow moth.

The southern section of this SSSI includes the most important breeding site for the nightingale in Kent. Around Wouldham there are a number of areas of freshwater marsh with dykes dividing the fields: Over 60 species of bird have been recorded in this area

including sedge and reed warbler, skylark and yellowhammer. Nearing Rochester the presence of plants such as sea clover, sea milkwort and sea spurrey indicates the salinity of the water.

Baty's Marsh

Baty's Marsh (formerly known as Borstal Marsh) was designated as a Local Nature Reserve (LNR) by Rochester upon Medway City Council in August 1987. It is a prominent site whether viewed downstream from Rochester city centre, or from the Strood side of the river, or the North Downs Way,

which runs across the M2 motorway bridge. It affords excellent views over the Medway Estuary.

The site is considered to be of county wildlife importance by the Kent Trust for Nature Conservation, and for this reason it has been included within the 'River Medway between Cuxton and Temple Marsh' Site of Nature Conservation Interest (SNCI). Baty's Marsh is a typical example of fragmented saltmarsh within the north Kent marshes. It is intersected by winding channels which fill up at high tide. This type of habitat has a very restricted distribution

Tidal reed bed (MRP)

around the shores of the British Isles and this heightens the importance of all remaining areas.

Although the site is small it is of international importance for wildlife. Its situation in the narrower part of the Medway Estuary, though still tidal, is more influenced by the freshwater content of the river and makes the site of added interest. The long-term stability of this saltmarsh has given rise to a diverse saltmarsh flora and fauna.

There is a small but significant area of mud which is exposed at low tide. The marsh is backed by a narrow belt of scrub and

predominately rough grassland. Various species of bird visit the saltmarsh in the winter, and breed in the scrub during the summer months. The site also supports a number of rare invertebrates.

Although the site does provide a feeding area and roost for some of the estuarine birds which frequent the north Kent marshes, the ornithological value of Baty's Marsh is thought to be diminished somewhat by the constant disturbance to the mudflats caused by the proximity of moored boats to the north and east.

Clover, yellow rattle, bugle and bittercups

Medway Valley Walk logo

The design of the Medway Valley Walk logo features the kingfisher, a native bird of the River Medway.

A flash of sapphire is all that is needed to identify this bird as it streaks above the river or dives to snatch a minnow. This most brilliantly coloured of British birds is largely confined to the banks of rivers and streams because of its diet: minnows, sticklebacks and gudgeon, also water beetles, dragonfly nymphs and other water creatures. Its bright colouring is a defensive adaptation; predators have learnt to leave the bird alone because its flesh is foul-tasting.

It fishes with a shallow dive from a perch or from a hovering position, and beats its catch on a branch before bolting it down, head first. A fish swallowed tail first would choke the bird as its fins and scales opened; so a kingfisher carries a fish by its tail only when the fish is going to be presented to another bird.

The kingfisher excavates its nest-hole in a river bank, sand or gravel pit.

Land Use

The character of the
Medway valley is
influenced by the
land use. Agriculture in the
Medway valley and across the
river's catchment area tends
largely to be mixed in
character. It includes both
arable land and pasture with
orchards and woodland. The
High Weald area in particular
still supports a
typically
traditional
agricultural
landscape of
small fields
and hedgerows
interspersed
with small
shaws and
relic
woodlands.
Dairying, as
part of a mixed farming
regime, is more predominant
here than further
downstream.

Museum of Kent Life

The middle reaches of the
river tend to be the most
intensively farmed. Much of
the area between Tonbridge
and Yalding and south to
Paddock Wood is covered
with a fine loamy soil called
brickearth, deposited by
glacial meltwaters. This,
together with the alluvial soils
deposited by the river, is the
reason for the highly fertile
agricultural land in parts of
this area. Beyond Yalding
limy sands and clays
associated with the
Greensand are added to the
alluvium, again creating
fertile soils.

The cultivated land along the
course of the river produces
mainly cereals and
horticultural products
together with orchards and
some hops. Horticulture, a
particular feature in the
river's catchment area
between Tonbridge and
Maidstone, has expanded in
some areas at the expense of
orchards and hops. However,
although the number of
orchards has declined, this is
still an important aspect of
farming particularly in areas

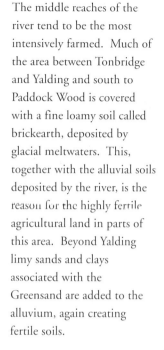

such as that between Yalding
and Maidstone.

Hop gardens are also a
disappearing feature of the
agricultural industry with
changes in demand,
competition from abroad and
other economic factors. The
one-time extent of this
industry is evident in the
number of oast houses to be
seen along parts of Medway
Valley and some of its
tributaries. Most of these are
now converted to private
dwellings.

More pastureland, mainly
improved or semi-improved,
tends to be upstream from
Tonbridge. Dairying, for
example, is much less a
feature of farming east of
Tonbridge.

With intensive agriculture so
predominant along much of
the Medway valley, there are
few areas of major
significance in wildlife
conservation terms. One
important exception is the
marshes and unimproved
grasslands between
Holborough and Burham.
This area has been designated
an SSSI.

Woodlands tend to occur as small fragments along the river's course, relics of once much larger areas of woodland. Some of the smaller tributary valleys crossing the Hastings Beds and Greensand are also wooded. Some of these woods support a rich wildlife community including species that indicate the woodland is ancient in origin. Those few woodlands still actively managed are largely under a coppice regime.

Coppice Woodlands

Nearly all the woods along the Medway valley, as in the rest of England, have been modified and managed by people. Sweet chestnut is the most popular species grown and for centuries the timber has provided material for fencing, hop poles, buildings and pulp for paper-making.

Coppicing is the process of cutting back sweet chestnut stems on a regular cycle (normally of 15 years); from the remaining stump, called a stool, the chestnut regrows very quickly and so may be harvested again 15 years on. Sadly, the market for coppice has decreased significantly over recent years and some coppice woodlands are no longer being managed.

Mineral Extraction

Open water is quite a significant habitat in the river's catchment area. This is not only a result of the widespread extraction industry but also includes reservoirs like that at Bough Beech west of Tonbridge.

Aggregates used in the construction industry are extensively quarried along parts of the river's course, including alluvial sands and gravels. Many of these quarries and pits have been worked out or have become disused for other reasons. Some have since been flooded to create attractive landscape features and important sites for wildfowl and other wildlife. Some have also been developed for recreational use.

At Tonbridge, for example, Haysden Country Park created along the Medway

Ragwort

includes a disused gravel pit, now an important recreational feature of the park. Further upstream another flooded pit is occupied by a sailing club. Where recreational use is limited the wildlife value increases with less visitor disturbance.

Brookland Lake, on the west bank of the river near Snodland, and the lakes adjacent to it are another example of open water providing both recreational facilities and wildlife habitat and adding to the diversity of scenery found along the course of the River Medway.

Iron-making

Historically the importance of the area lay in its relatively rich and accessible iron deposits. These were exploited on a small-scale in the Iron Age. In Roman times the ore was heated by charcoal in a clay-walled mound through which air was forced by bellows. The Ashdown Forest and the High Weald supplied abundant timber for fuel.

After several centuries of decline the industry was revived in Tudor times when the more sophisticated blast furnaces introduced by the French were pioneered on the headstreams of the Medway.

The process produced cast iron which was forged into wrought iron. The steep Wealden streams proved ideal for impounding as 'furnace' or 'hammer' ponds to provide a head of water to drive the twin waterwheels characteristic of Tudor forges. These drove furnace bellows and trip hammers to forge the iron.

Quarrying

Another important product of the Medway valley was Kentish ragstone. This was quarried by the Romans in the Maidstone area and transported to London to build the city walls. The Normans continued the process, ferrying ragstone from the Isle of Grain to build the Tower of London. Kentish ragstone is still used by the Environment Agency to build tidal defences. Its workmen continue the traditional skills of shaping the rocks to interlock into a durable defence without the need for mortar.

North of Maidstone there are extensive chalk quarries as a component of the cement industry.

History and Archaeology

The name of the river may derive from the Celtic word medu, meaning mead, presumably signifying a river with 'sweet' water. The Romans called the river Fluminus Meduwaeias and the Saxons knew it as the Medwaeg.

Early History

The fertile soils of the Medway valley have been an important focus for settlement from earliest times, many Neolithic long barrows having been found along the valley, as well as evidence of later settlements of the Bronze and Iron Ages. Aylesford was one of the most significant of these settlements as the gravel here

High level view of Teston Lock

afforded a convenient river crossing and there were well drained sites available for colonisation. The river valley was well populated in Roman times with several villa sites along the lower river, including the large complex at Eccles. Ragstone, iron and corn were carried by water from Kent at this time, but road transport was also important and three major crossings were built over the Medway - at the estuary for Watling Street, and on the sites of Maidstone for the Hythe road and Tonbridge for the Rye road.

The river continued to be a focus for settlement through the Anglo-Saxon period, with

East Farleigh Bridge

many villages along its course being associated with meadowland. At the end of the era the Domesday book recorded numerous mill and fishery sites along both the main channel and its tributaries. Rochester was the only large urban settlement on the Medway at the time, it being one of eight boroughs recorded for Kent, and there was already a castle associated with the town.

Medieval Period

By the medieval period the mills and fish weirs were being viewed as obstructions by the newly emerging merchant class who wanted to use the river for navigation. Legislation was passed to try and enforce their removal, starting with Magna Carta, in which it was decreed that 'all fish weirs shall be removed from the Thames, the Medway, and

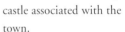

throughout the whole of England, except on the sea coast'. The battle was a protracted one and in 1423 commissions were still being set up to review the situation. On the Medway they were only concerned with the river up to the bridge at Maidstone, this being viewed as the limit of navigation at the time.

Among the main outgoing cargoes were timber, carried

across country to Maidstone, wool and corn, although for all these products the main route was still via the south coast ports of Kent and Sussex. Ragstone from the Maidstone area was more local to the navigation and was carried by river to London, where it was used, for example, in the building of Westminster Abbey and Eton College. Rochester continued to be the dominant port but from the

14th century Maidstone evolved as the market for the rich agricultural land surrounding it, and for goods carried across country from the Weald. Boats serving Maidstone were restricted in size and needed to have stowable masts to negotiate Rochester and Aylesford bridges. Upstream from Maidstone, boats were able to reach Yalding, at least from the 1580s, and this also developed as a staging post.

Attempts to extend the Navigation

By the 17th century both Rochester and Maidstone had populations of about three thousand each, while Tonbridge 16 miles further upstream had only between five and eight hundred inhabitants and the villages in between were even smaller. Tonbridge, on the Rye road, became a market for the cloth and iron industries of the Weald and this, together with the demands of the Navy dockyards for timber and ordnance from the Weald, prompted schemes to extend

the navigation. A further impetus came with the diversification of agriculture in the valley after the introduction of hops and orchard fruit, as well as market garden produce; all required a speedy delivery to market.

In 1600 a dispute arose between the ironmasters trying to use the navigation and the owners of land next to the river in Maidstone who wanted to retain their mills and weirs. As the area under concern was upstream of East Farleigh this was above the tidal limit, and it was held that this part of the river was not therefore navigable by right; although

Medway at Allington

some obstructions were removed no right to navigation was established. A further dispute occurred in 1627 when the need to get timber and ordnance to the Navy was becoming acute as the country was at war with both France and Spain. Although this was the overt reason for clearing the navigation, there may also have been the intention to raise money independently of Parliament as Charles I was attempting to grant a monopoly to the undertaker.

The Act of 1627 was thrown out by Parliament but by 1664 much had changed. It was in this year that an Act was passed to extend the navigation of the Medway. By this time the main industries of the Weald, clothmaking and ironworking, were in decline, but there was at the same time an expansion and diversification of agriculture. Again, however, the motives for the Act were not clear-cut, and the proposed navigation was once more granted as a monopoly, this

time to Royalist supporters who were seen to have suffered during the parliamentary period. They do not seem to have been able to raise the initial capital and only minimal works were carried out. It is also interesting to note that opposers of the Act, whatever their stated views, were mainly Parliamentarians.

Extension of the Navigation to Tonbridge

The undertakers listed for the second Act for the upper Medway of 1739 were of a very different nature, far more business-like, and between them taking up shares in a joint stock company. The stated aim was to extend the navigation as far as Forest Row, although it was probably never actually envisaged to take it further than Tonbridge. When navigation had been completed that far the company would hold jurisdiction over the newly navigable, non-tidal stretch of the river. The company undertook only one major

cut on the river at Yalding, but installed 14 locks between Maidstone and Tonbridge and carried out major alterations to bridges along its course. The works were completed by the 1760s.

The Medway, being in the south of the country, is in an area of light rainfall, generally less than 30 inches per year falling over much of the catchment area. The rocks along the river, predominantly Mesozoic and Tertiary are of a water-bearing nature, and although this helps to even out the flow there are still found to be dramatic rises and falls,

especially in winter. In general the stream level tends to reflect weather conditions prevailing a short time previously. This had a significant impact on trying to maintain trade, as did the restrictive size of the locks on the upper river. These could accommodate only vessels with a maximum length of 65 feet and beam of $15\frac{1}{2}$ feet, and as only a bow hauling path had been built they would have been pulled by men not horses. The small craft that were developed were built to the maximum size possible and had rudders that could be stowed alongside in the

View of the fertile hills above Yalding

Floating reeds

restricted space of the locks; they were known as 'snapphatchers'.

Other Navigation Schemes

Several schemes were put forward to extend the navigation of the Medway beyond Tonbridge, and to link it with other rivers in the south-east, but were not carried out. The most ambitious, the Grand Southern Canal, proposed in 1810, would have linked the Medway with the Arun in Sussex. Acts were passed and work carried out, however, to improve the lower river from Maidstone downstream to the estuary. Under the first Act of 1792 only widening and dredging took place, but there were two further Acts, in 1802, under which Allington lock and lockhouse were built, and in 1824, under which a horse towpath was constructed from Maidstone to Rochester, three cuts made and Aylesford bridge altered. The works made Maidstone Lock on the upper navigation redundant although it was not removed until 1881.

The lower river also saw the only junction canal to be completed between the Medway and the Thames. This was proposed in 1800 but was not completed until 1824. This seems to have been an ill-fated venture as little advantage accrued from the gain in distance as the tides still limited the journey time to London. By the 1840s river navigations were beginning to face competition from rail, especially for freight, and the canal was in fact bought out by the South East Railway Company, and the tunnel between Higham and Strood used for their rail track along the north Kent coast.

Trade on the Medway in the 19th Century

Rail competition impinged on the trade of the whole river increasingly during the second half of the 19th century, but in its heyday barges had carried on a thriving trade. Maidstone developed as the main upper Medway port, with additional wharves being added along the river downstream of the bridge in the town centre. The barges coming only this far could be larger than those employed on the upper river, although they still required stowable masts to negotiate the bridges. Although timber and iron had been envisaged as the main cargoes, it was imported coal from the north that actually dominated trade. Agricultural products, especially corn, fruit and hops were the main outgoing trade, together with some timber, ragstone, paper and bricks. From the late 19th century cement was also an important freight from the lower river. As well as the boats of the Maidstone wharfingers and the Upper Medway Navigation Company, the growing brick and cement companies built their own barge fleets, and as the industries were concentrated on the lower river these vessels could be of a larger size. Industries of the upper river, which included gunpowder manufacture and seed crushing, were disadvantaged by the restrictive size of the navigation and were moved elsewhere.

Twentieth Century

By the close of the 19th century much of the trade of the river had been diverted to rail. Two very modern preoccupations were also emerging as concerns: the increasing use of the river for recreational use and pollution of the river from urban and industrial sources. The continued opening of locks for pleasure craft to pass, the increasing abstraction of water for domestic and industrial supplies, together with the deterioration of the infrastructure, led to increasing difficulties in maintaining the navigation above Maidstone. Flooding at the turn of the century seems to have been especially severe and further exacerbated the situation. The Upper Medway Company finally ceased trading in 1905, despite an Act passed in 1892 to try and remedy their financial position.

This left the upper river with no controlling body until the Medway Conservancy Board

Redundant church at Allington

was set up in 1911. They carried out improvements to the navigation, enlarging the lock size to 105 by $22^1/_2$ feet, and removing three locks that were no longer viewed as necessary. Despite these works, trade was not resuscitated and in fact became even more concentrated on the industrial stretch of the lower river. Eventually, however, most of the industry was closed down or moved to more accessible sites on the Thames. In 1934 the Conservancy was wound up and replaced by the River

Medway Catchment Board, later to be superseded by the Kent River Authority on the upper river and the Medway Ports Authority for the lower river. Under the former the restriction on opening of the lock gates by boat owners was removed in the 1960s, thus allowing for the great increase in use of the river above Maidstone by pleasure craft. The National Rivers Authority held jurisdiction over the upper river from 1989. The NRA was replaced by the Environment Agency in 1996.

Flood Defence

The impermeable clay and the large areas of urban development give the river its flashy character, making the EA's flood defence role of paramount importance.

Historically the Medway valley and Eden valley suffered flooding of both agricultural land and property. Many of the clay and alluvial sections of the river's course quickly became water saturated in winter months and at times of heavy rainfall. Extremes of flow may vary five hundredfold between summer and winter.

In September 1968 the worst flood in living memory occurred, causing massive damage both in the town of Tonbridge and in the downstream areas.

In order to alleviate flooding, a flood storage area was created above Tonbridge at Leigh and is now operated by the EA. This is the largest on-river flood storage area in the UK. In times of heavy rainfall three gates in an earthen embankment across the river regulate the amount of flood water passing downstream to Tonbridge. Some of the run-off is held back, forming a temporary lake whenever the flows exceed the channel capacities through the town. The 'lake' can be drained at a controlled

rate once flood flows have abated.

Information from flow gauging stations, level recorders and rain gauges in the catchment is telemetered to a control room so that flow through the gates can be regulated.

Between Leigh and the tidal limit at Allington there are ten navigational locks and accompanying flood control sluices. Nine have by-pass channels with automatic high capacity sluices which maintain a constant upstream level and take surplus flows. Six of these have radial gates finely balanced by a counterweight on the end of

an arm. A device with a float-like action is attached to the arm causing it to tip the balance when water levels rise. The gate then opens until water levels fall and the 'float' resumes its original position. Three other sluices have vertically operated gates which are electrically powered. The tenth lock has hand-operated rack and pinion tumbler sluices but were modernised in 1991.

The EA sluice and lock keepers trim levels and operate Allington Lock and the lifting bridge at Yalding. A hydraulic dredger is operated by the Agency all year round to clear blockages and shoals.

Sluice Weir near East Peckham

History of the Medway Navigation

1531 'Commissioners of Sewers' were established to improve land drainage and prevent flooding. The Medway Commissioners also proposed to clear the river for navigation, 'so that its natural course is unobstructed and her Majesty's subjects can travel along it in boats as a highway with cars.'

1624 Further moves were made to make the river navigable to transport oak trees from the Weald to Chatham for ship building. The weirs and a low bridge at Nettlestead seem to have stopped this scheme.

1664 The first specific Navigation Act gave powers for certain 'undertakers' to erect, build, set-up and make locks, weirs, turnpikes, pens of water, wharfs and cranes to load and unload iron, ordnance balls, timber and other materials.

1739 A second Act was passed to make the river navigable to Forest Row. Locks were built between Maidstone and Tonbridge by 1746. The 'Company of the Proprietors of the Navigation of the River Medway' transported materials down river for the Navy and corn, hops, coal and lime upstream.

1828 James Christie was engaged as canal engineer to plan an extension from Tonbridge to Penshurst. He asked for special rates for his own barges and purchased Tonbridge Town Mills to control the water rights. His draining of the Town Pen in 1829, which stranded all barges at the wharfs, resulted in legal and physical battles which bankrupted him.

1842 The railway brought competition to river transport. In 1882 a new navigation company was formed but fell into receivership by 1910.

1911 The prospect of the river becoming derelict led to the creation of the Medway Conservancy Board. The Navigation between Maidstone and Tonbridge was re-opened in 1915.

1934 Powers were taken over by the River Medway catchment Board under the 1930 Land Drainage Act. Successor bodies were the Kent River Board and the Kent River Authority.

1974 Responsibility for the Navigation was transferred to the Southern Water Authority. Commercial traffic had ceased, but the water remained popular for pleasure boats.

1989 The Water Act invested responsibility for the Navigation in the National Rivers Authority. A restoration and maintenance programme ensures that it will continue to be enjoyed by boat owners, anglers, ramblers and the general public

River Bridges

Great Bridge, Tonbridge

A three-span brick arch bridge was built in 1814 to carry the High Street over the Medway after the previous bridge had been destroyed by a flood. It was narrow and a cantilevered footway on cast-iron brackets was added to the downstream face in 1886, but the bridge was unsatisfactory and three years later the arches were removed and replaced by cast-iron beams supported by concrete piers on the old foundations. The bridge was widened in 1925/27 from 34 feet in width to 55 feet by the addition of a reinforced concrete section on the upstream side. Now, in order to meet current loading requirements, the cast-iron beams have been replaced by steel ones. An attractive feature of the bridge is its cast-iron railings.

The overall span of 75 feet is made up of three spans of 23 feet with two three feet wide piers. The water clearance is seven feet.

Cannon Bridge, Tonbridge

This is a three-span bridge of approximately equal spans, 122 feet in length and 52 feet wide, built in 1969 to carry the Tonbridge by-pass to the east of the town. The bridge is constructed with pre-stressed concrete beams with an in-situ concrete deck and has two-feet wide concrete piers.

Hartlake Bridge near Golden Green

This bridge was built in 1910 by the Tonbridge Rural District Council and is an early example of a reinforced concrete bridge. It is a through-bridge in that the 16 feet wide carriageway is carried between the two 9 feet 6 inches concrete side beams. The river span is 67 feet between the 4 feet 6 inches square concrete piers and there is a side span on the north bank 36 feet long. Concrete repairs were carried out in 1982 and the bridge

was strengthened by stitching steel rods diagonally between the piers and the beams.

Branbridges, East Peckham

This is a three-span bridge at a 47 degree skew to the B2015, which at this point is built on a causeway. There are two five-feet wide masonry piers with a 24 feet wide central navigational channel and two weired flood channels 18 feet wide. It was originally built about 1904 with cast iron beams and patent flooring plates, but has recently been rebuilt with steel beams, a reinforced concrete deck and parapets in Kentish ragstone.

Railway Bridge, Branbridges

The Paddock Wood to Maidstone West railway line crosses the Medway by means of a riveted steel truss bridge, a typical Southern Railway design. Wind bracing is provided by four lattice girders which tie the top flanges together. This was the first railway line to Maidstone and was opened in 1844 by the South Eastern Railway and joins the main London to Dover line at Paddock Wood.

Twyford Bridge, Yalding

This bridge links Yalding and East Peckham, crossing the River Medway and its tributary, the Teise. The earliest record of it is in 1325 when an inquisition was held to discover who was responsible for repairs. It was later mentioned in 1475 as benefiting from the Wills of John Church and Richard Paritt. It is constructed from Kentish ragstone and has five arches up to 16 feet 9 inches in span with large angular buttresses which are carried up to form refuges above. One of the arches is a flood arch which may well have been added later. The overall length of the bridge is 300 feet, with the carriageway only 12 feet wide between the parapets which are a later addition built in red brickwork. Substantial repairs to the parapets were carried out in 1903 and extensive accident repairs have been completed recently.

Teston Bridge

Bow Bridge, Wateringbury

In 1914/15 the present bridge was built to replace an old dilapidated wooden bridge and also to increase the navigational clearance by two feet. The bridge has nine spans of 30 feet, five over the river and four over the flood plain, with a width between parapets of 18 feet. It was built of reinforced concrete, then a material in its early days, with the idea of saving on maintenance costs. However, problems of concrete spalling soon arose and the bridge has suffered from this problem for much of its life. A four-ton weight restriction was imposed in 1968, but it was decided to retain the bridge. In 1981 major repairs were carried out which included the removal of the concrete parapets and their replacement by steel railings. Originally the bridge was constructed for the Maidstone Rural District Council but it was taken over by the county in 1916.

Teston Bridge

This bridge, constructed of Kentish ragstone, originally had seven arches, three over the river and four flood arches. The date of its construction is unknown, probably 15th century or earlier, although there is a record in 1526 of a legacy to help pay for repairs. The large pointed centre arch was rebuilt in 1793 to improve navigation, and the four flood arches were reduced to three during extensive repairs in 1830. Between most of the arches are cutwaters which are carried up to form pedestrian refuge recesses in the parapet above. The bridge is 216 feet long with the arches up to 24 feet 6 inches in span and a carriageway 11 feet 6 inches wide. The bridge is a listed structure.

Barming Bridge

This old river crossing site is occupied by a three-span wooden bridge with timber piers encased in concrete for strengthening. It has a single carriageway with a three-ton weight restriction and the bridge is closed to traffic when the Medway is in flood.

Barming Bridge (Kettle Bridge)

East Farleigh Bridge

The first record of this 300-feet long bridge was in 1324 when an inquisition was held to discover who was responsible for its upkeep. It is constructed of Kentish ragstone and has four pointed arches with spans of between 24 feet and 26 feet 3 inches, and a fifth pointed arch 13 feet wide added later to accommodate a tow path. The four larger arches each have four chamfered stone ribs to their soffits. Despite the narrow carriageway of 11 feet 6 inches, there are no pedestrian refuges. At the southern end the road is carried at an angle of nearly 45% to the south-west by a small pointed arch springing from near the crown of the adjacent river arch. During the 15th and 16th centuries the bridge was owned by the Culpepper family, but during the 17th century the parishes of Barming and East Farleigh became responsible for its maintenance until it was taken over by the County in 1646. During the Civil War General Fairfax with the Parliamentary Army crossed the bridge, turning the flank of the Kentish Royalists, and captured Maidstone. The bridge is a listed structure.

Tovil Bridge

In 1886 a bridge carrying a railway goods line to Tovil was opened on this site, but little remains now except one abutment and traces of an embankment. There was also a rivetted iron footbridge, but this was replaced in 1984 by the present bridge built on the original abutments. It is a welded steel truss bridge with a curved upper chord and has a span of 100 feet and a width of 6 feet.

Maidstone Town Bridge

This handsome Victorian bridge is at the site of the old river crossing at Maidstone. The first known bridge was a wooden one built in Saxon times which remained in use until it was replaced by a stone bridge with five arches in the 14th century. In 1808 this bridge was widened, but it became unsafe and was replaced by the present one in 1879. This bridge is a masonry arch bridge with three spans, each arch being constructed with blocks of Cornish granite in a single ring. The spandrels and parapets are of Kentish ragstone, capped with granite. It is 287 feet in length, originally 40 feet wide but widened by 20 feet in 1927; the widening can be seen on the arch underneath. Sir Joseph Bazalgette, of London main drainage fame, was the engineer.

St Peter's Bridge, Maidstone

This pleasing bridge has the appearance of being a flat arch. Structurally it is a single span portal frame bridge with the stresses being concentrated in the haunches, while the legs are

concealed and supported on piles. It consists of a number of pre-cast concrete units, tensioned together to form beams with an in-situ concrete deck. The bridge has a span of 197 feet, width of 56 feet, and was built in 1976.

Maidstone East Railway Bridge

This is a steel girder truss bridge carrying the Swanley to Ashford railway line and a footpath across the Medway near Maidstone East railway station. It replaced the original bridge in 1927 when the line was upgraded to take boat trains. The railway was built by the London, Chatham and Dover Railway,

opened to Maidstone in 1874 and to Ashford in 1884.

New works have recently been completed replacing the railway viaduct on the east side by a bridge. This is to allow the A229 spine road to run along the river bank and to pass under the railway.

M20 Bridges

The upstream bridge was built in 1960 to carry the old M20 over the Medway; it has three spans of 55, 134 and 80 feet and is 81 feet in width with a water clearance of 28 feet. It was built making use of prestressed precast concrete units and in-situ concrete. It is asymmetrical both in

appearance and design as both cantilevered and suspended spans are used. It now carries only west bound traffic. Engineer: Scott, Wilson, Kirkpatrick & Partners.

East bound traffic is carried on the new bridge, completed in 1993, which has three spans of 117, 205 and 117 feet. It is a steel bridge with the reinforced concrete deck acting compositely with the steel beams. These are laid as continuous members over the piers, thus reducing the bending moments and the amount of steel required. In order to reduce maintenance costs, the beams are made of 'weathering steel' which rusts to form a protective coating and does not require painting. Engineer: Travers Morgan. Contractor: Balfour Beatty.

Aylesford Bridge

Aylesford has been a major crossing place for centuries and at the ford in 455 AD a battle occurred between Hengist and Horsa. The first bridge was probably a timber

one, but in 1370 it was found to be broken and a new bridge with seven pointed arches was built in Kentish ragstone. It was paid for by the alms of those crossing it. It was rebuilt in 1670 by Sir William Sidley and became the responsibility of the County to maintain.

In 1824 the two centre arches were replaced by a single elliptical arch by the Lower Medway Navigation to give greater headroom under the bridge for vessels. Massive buttresses were constructed on either side of the new arch and provided with cantilevered pedestrian refuges. Similar refuges exist above the triangular cutwaters of the original piers to the north of the main span. The bridge is 310 feet in length with six arches ranging from 13 feet 6 inches to 60 feet 6 inches in span, and is 13 feet wide. Today the bridge carries one-way traffic into the village with the return traffic carried by a Bailey-type bridge upstream. The bridge is a listed structure.

M2 Medway Bridge

This is a massive reinforced concrete structure with an overall length of 3,272 feet, width 113 feet and a river clearance of 100 feet. The main river span is 500 feet with two equal side spans of 312 feet, in addition there is an 11 span western approach viaduct of 1,350 feet and an eastern one of 7 spans 792 feet in length. The bridge was founded on chalk either by the use of piles or by spread footings. In the construction of the approaches 162 pre-stressed beams, up to 132 feet in length, were cast on site and erected on the piers by means of a launching girder. The bridge itself was built by cantilevering the two main beams out from both sides of the two river piers in 10 feet increments, with each section being tied back to the previous one by steel bars before proceeding with the next one. In order to keep the work in balance the side spans were carried on temporary support towers, the centre spans being cantilevered 200 feet out over

the river. To complete the 500 feet centre span and join the two halves of the bridge together, a 100 feet freely supported span was erected sitting on the ends of the cantilevered sections. Engineer: Freeman, Fox & Partners. Contractor: Kier, Christianu & Nielson.

The Medway Bridge, completed in 1964, is to be

strengthened to enable it to carry the current highway loading. Also, it will be altered to carry east-bound traffic only as part of the proposed M2 widening. West-bound traffic will cross the Medway by a new bridge to be built immediately upstream; adjacent to this will be the Channel Tunnel Railway Bridge, although there is a possibility that

there will be a combined bridge.

Rochester Bridges

The lowest practicable crossing point on the River Medway was at Rochester and here Roman military engineers constructed the first bridge. After the Romans left, the bridge fell into disrepair until the Saxons built a wooden bridge

M2 Motorway Bridge near Rochester

making use of the remains of the stone piers in 960 AD. Then, for 400 years, bridges of this type suffered destruction and repair until 1387 when two local knights commenced work on a stone bridge. This was built 40 yards upstream of the existing bridge opposite to what is now the offices of the Rochester Bridge Trust. The bridge, 566 feet long and 15 feet wide with ten arches, remained in use for 469 years, although it was improved in 1820 by Rennie who widened it, rounded the arches, turned the two centre arches into one and provided stone balustrading.

A new bridge, however, was required and work started in 1850 on a three-span bridge with cast-iron arches 610 feet in length and 40 feet wide, designed by William Cubitt. It was founded on 70 six and seven feet diameter cast-iron cylinders which were sunk into the river bed by the use of compressed air, a first for bridge foundations. Excavation inside the cylinders was hard and

arduous on account of the debris from ancient bridges, as the bridge was being built back on the old line of Watling Street. When the bridge was opened in 1856, the medieval bridge was blown up in a spectacular explosion by the Royal Engineers, the balustrading being saved and re-erected along the Esplanade. River traffic was considerable and with the low clearance under the arches they suffered damage. To alleviate this the bridge was rebuilt during 1910-14 on the existing piers by removing the arches and replacing them by the existing hogged back steel trust bridge.

Concurrently with the construction of William Cubitt's road bridge, Joseph Cubitt, his son, was building a railway bridge for the East Kent Railway (later the London, Chatham & Dover Railway (LCDR) immediately downstream. This was opened for train services in 1858 between Strood and Faversham and from Victoria to Dover in 1861.

Following the amalgamation of the Southern Eastern Railway (SER) and the LCDR in 1899, there was a rationalisation of services and since 1922 all trains

passing through Rochester have used the SER steel lattice girder bridge built in 1891 next to the LCDR bridge. This bridge was kept in being until 1967 when it was demolished and on the piers a three-lane road bridge, carried on twin steel box girders, was built to carry east-bound traffic. It was opened in 1970 with the existing road bridge being altered to take the west-bound traffic.

The road bridges are owned and maintained by the Rochester Bridge Trust, founded in 1398.

Walk Planning and Preparation

Walking Advice

No season of the year is closed to walkers; enjoyment can be gained from walking on a bright crisp winter's morning or on an 'Indian Summer's' day in the autumn. Equally rewarding is a springtime walk when the countryside is full of new life and growth.

Always wear suitable clothing and footwear for the season. Be prepared for changeable weather. Take clothes which are warm and waterproof. Inexpensive overtrousers will give protection from any discomfort caused by walking through high vegetation or rain-drenched crops.

Sections of paths may be muddy after periods of rain so wear strong, comfortable and waterproof footwear.

Allow plenty of time to complete your chosen walk. Reckon on walking 2 or $2^1/_2$ miles (3.2 or 4 km) an hour. The distances and times for each section of the walk are shown on the route maps, and in the information. Allow more time if it has been wet, if you are elderly, or have children or inexperienced walkers with you.

The route has been established in consultation with landowners and farmers and follows public rights of way and permissive paths. Remember that most public paths cross private estates and farmland. Some evolved as routes from farms to the nearest village and were not designed for large numbers of people. Sometimes you are walking through a place of work; enjoy the countryside but please have regard for its life and work. Crops and animals are the farmers' livelihood and should be left undisturbed.

Always keep to the path to avoid trespass. When faced with a growing crop you may have to seek a way around the edge of the field even though in law the landowner or farmer is required to keep the footpath clear. Walk in single file through a crop. It is useful to carry secateurs to help clear the way if a path has become overgrown. You may remove any obstruction on a right of way - sufficient only to allow you to proceed.

Take care when crossing or walking along country roads. Keep to the right, in single file, facing oncoming traffic. On a bend, however, walk on the outside and keep a good lookout for traffic.

Remember to leave things as found - refasten gates you find closed. Straying stock can cause damage and an expensive inconvenience to farmers. Always use gates and stiles to negotiate fences and hedges.

Take your litter home - it can injure people, animals and wildlife. Guard against all risk of fire, especially in dry weather. Picnicking is not permitted on private land; you only have a right of passage on a right of way.

To avoid injury or distress to farm animals and wildlife, keep dogs under control at all times. If not on a lead they can run surprisingly long distances and consequently out of sight of the owner. Please keep dogs on leads, particularly when passing through fruit growing areas or fields with standing crops. Farmers have a right to shoot dogs found worrying their livestock.

Distant view of Greensand hills near East Peckham

Using the Guidebook

This book is designed to be a practical guide to walking the Medway Valley Walk in either direction. It is a guidebook including a route guide. It may be used intact or separately by carefully removing the weather resistant route guide from the centre of the book. The guidebook contains a route description, specialist and other information and guidance on planning and preparing for a walk. The route guide, with information about features passed en route, is self-contained and can be used independently of the guidebook.

The route maps have been arranged in sequence from Tonbridge to Rochester. When walking from south to north, the book is used in a conventional way, whilst the north to south route is read from the back of the book to the front.

By carefully folding it back, the book and/or route guide will fit into a map case, thus providing protection against damage, dirt and damp.

Because the countryside is constantly changing, with stiles, gates and field boundaries being removed or new ones erected, there are no route directions. Route finding should not be a problem given the large scale route maps and the extensive waymarking and signing on the ground.

Ordnance Survey

This page is sponsored by Ordnance Survey

Maps

Ordnance Survey sheet number and titles

Landranger Series, scale 1:50,000 - $1\frac{1}{4}$ inches to 1 mile (2 cm to 1 km)

❖ 188 Maidstone and The Weald of Kent

❖ 178 The Thames Estuary

Pathfinder Series, scale 1:25,000 - $2\frac{1}{2}$ inches to 1 mile (4 cm to 1 km)

❖ 1228 Tonbridge and Edenbridge

❖ 1229 Paddock Wood and Staplehurst

❖ 1209 Maidstone

❖ 1193 Chatham and Meopham

Ordnance Survey maps are available from local tourist information centres and bookshops, and direct from Kent County Council. Planning Department, Springfield, Maidstone, Kent ME14 2LX.

Grid References

The grid references of interesting features on or near the route of the Medway Valley Walk are given in the narrative text.

The framework of squares spaced at one kilometre intervals over all Ordnance Survey maps is known as the National Grid. The grid facilitates the pinpointing of any place in the country, giving it a unique reference number.

To give a reference number, first take the western (left-hand) edge of the kilometre square in which the place lies.

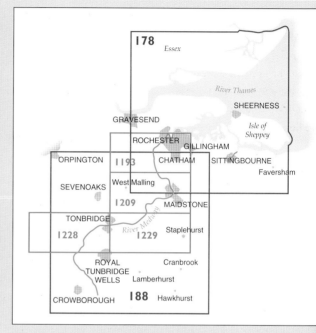

Read the figures at the end of the line in the top and bottom margins of the map, then moving eastwards (to the right) estimate the position of the place in tenths across the square.

Secondly, take the southern edge of the same square and read the figures at the end of the line in the side margins of the map. Then, moving northwards, estimate the position of the place in tenths up the square. This gives a six figure reference number accurate to within 100 metres.

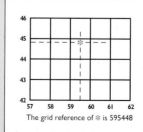

The grid reference of ✳ is 595448

In finding out a grid reference, the first three numbers of the six figure number refer to the line and number of tenths across the square, whilst the second three numbers refer to the line and number of tenths up the square.

Route Options

The Medway Valley Walk is 28¼ miles (45.2 km) long and can be undertaken as a long-distance walk in one or more days, using the main and link routes.

If you wish to undertake the Medway Valley Walk in sections you need to be aware of problems of returning to your starting point. Possible solutions might be as follows:

a) Using two cars, one at the starting point and the other at the proposed finishing point.

b) Using one car and public transport. If relying on infrequent bus services it is suggested that you make your outward journey by bus thus returning confidently to your car or base.

c) Retracing your steps - the scenery can look surprisingly different when walking in the opposite direction.

The walk can be undertaken as a whole or in sections, with the following suggested itineraries:

Two days, approximately 14 miles (22.4 km) each, allow 7 hours.

Three days, approximately 9 miles (14.4 km) each, allow 4½ hours.

Four half-days, approximately 7 miles (11.2 km) each, allow 3½ hours.

Shorter walks can be devised by using the bus and rail routes which link with the following places along the route : Tonbridge, Golden Green (¾ mile - 1.2 km), East Peckham (½ mile - 0.8 km), Beltring (½ mile - 0.8 km), Yalding (⅔ mile - 1.1 km), Wateringbury (½ mile - 0.8 km), Teston (⅓ mile - 0.5 km), East Barming (¼ mile - 0.4 km), East Farleigh (¼ mile - 0.4 km), Maidstone, Aylesford, Wouldham, Rochester.

View of Medway valley from St Michael's churchyard, East Peckham

Waymarking and Signing

The term waymarking refers to marking objects along a public right of way. It complements signposting, which shows where a right of way leaves the metalled road and indicates its initial direction, and enables users to follow a path accurately and confidently at points where they might otherwise have difficulty.

Waymarking benefits not only users of rights of way but also farmers and landowners. It increases users' enjoyment of the countryside and helps to prevent unintentional trespass.

The Waymarking System

The recommended system in England and Wales uses small coloured arrows to show the direction of the path and also to act as a target when viewed from a distance. A different colour is used for each category of right of way:

❖ public rights of way that are footpaths are waymarked using yellow arrows;

❖ bridleways are waymarked with blue arrows;

❖ byways open to all traffic and other routes that may legally be used by wheeled vehicles are waymarked with red arrows, but they are intended only to show the status of the route and not to indicate whether it is physically suitable for vehicles.

If the status of a path changes along its length, so does the colour of the waymarking arrows. Where a right of way is part of a special route, such as a National Trail, Recreation Route or Circular Walk, the arrows are used in conjunction with the route's own symbol.

Transport

Car Parking

Places to park are shown on the route maps. Please note that these are not necessarily car parks. If a car park is not available, please park thoughtfully and sensibly to avoid causing an obstruction or damage to the roadside verges. Leave your car securely locked with valuables out of sight.

Bus and Train Services

It is not practical to give details of all the bus and train routes and services to and along the Medway Valley Walk, since they may change during the currency of this guidebook. Kent County Council publishes an annual Public Transport Map and Guide which contains comprehensive bus and rail route maps and lists of bus services and operators (see below).

For details of train services please telephone either (0345) 484950 or London (0171) 928 5100.

You are advised to check details of your journey before travelling, particularly with respect to Sunday services. Public transport information can be obtained from Kent County Council, Highways and Transportation Department, Springfield, Maidstone, Kent ME14 2LQ, telephone Freephone 0800 696996.

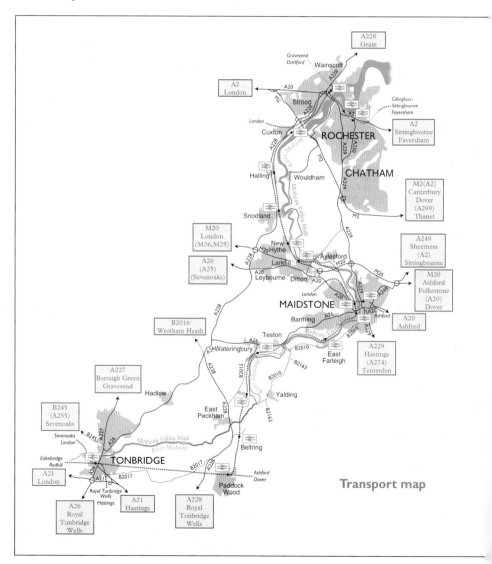

Transport map

Medway Valley Walk Questionnaire

In order to help us assess the success of the Medway Valley Walk we would like to hear your views about the route and the guidebook.

Please would you complete the questionnaire below and send it to the Access and Recreation Officer, Planning Department, Kent County Council, Springfield, Maidstone, Kent ME14 2LX. If you have borrowed this book from a library or friend, you may photocopy the questionnaire.

1. Which of these statements best describes you?

   I live close to the Medway Valley Walk ☐

   I came to the area specifically to walk the Medway Valley Walk ☐

   I did not come to the area specifically to walk the Medway Valley Walk ☐

2. Name of town/village where you live:

   ....

   ....

3. How did you first become aware of the Medway Valley Walk?

   Leaflet (which one) ☐

   ....

   Word-of-mouth ☐

   Saw sign or waymark ☐

   Advertising (where) ☐

   ....

   Newspaper (which one) ☐

   ....

   Other (write in) ☐

   ....

4. What influenced you to try the Medway Valley Walk?

   ....

   ....

   ....

5. Have you, or do you intend to:

   Walk all of the route in one go, or over a short period of time (eg one week) ☐

   Walk all of the route, in sections, over a longer period of time ☐

   Walk only sections of the route ☐

   Unlikely to walk any part of the route ☐

6. Which of the following modes of travel do you use to get to the start of your walk?

   Walk ☐

   Bus ☐

   Cycle ☐

   Train ☐

   Car ☐

   Other (write in) ☐

   ....

7. If you found the walk difficult to follow, what improvements would you like us to make, and where (please use grid references where possible)?

   ....

   ....

   ....

   ....

8. Please indicate the number of people in each category that accompanied you on your walk (including you):

Age	male	female
under 11	☐	☐
11-16	☐	☐
17-25	☐	☐
26-35	☐	☐
36-45	☐	☐
46-55	☐	☐
56-65	☐	☐
over 65	☐	☐

9. Would you recommend the Medway Valley Walk to anyone else?

Yes ☐

No ☐

If you answered "no" please tell us why you say that:

....
....
....
....

10. Where did you obtain this guidebook from?

Bookshop ☐

Tourist Information Centre ☐

Library ☐

Mail Order ☐

11. What do you like about the guidebook?

....
....
....
....
....

Is there anything you dislike about the guidebook?

....
....
....
....
....

12. How useful did you find the detachable route maps?

Easy to read and understand ☐

Satisfactory ☐

Difficult to follow ☐

Don't know ☐

13. Have you walked any section of these other routes?

North Downs Way ☐

Saxon Shore Way ☐

Greensand Way ☐

Wealdway ☐

Stour Valley Walk ☐

Elham Valley Way ☐

Darent Valley Path ☐

Eden Valley Walk ☐

High Weald Walk ☐

14. Are you a member of any of the following organisations? (please tick boxes)

Ramblers' Association ☐

National Trust ☐

RSPB ☐

Kent Trust for Nature Conservation ☐

Other walking or countryside organisations (write in) ☐

....
....

15. Are you a regular reader of any of the following publications for walkers?

The Great Outdoors ☐

Trail (Walker) ☐

Country Walking ☐

Other (write in) ☐

....
....

16. How do you gain information about walks and events in the countryside?

Local paper ☐

Tourist Information Centre ☐

Word-of-mouth ☐

Local radio ☐

District/County Council ☐

Library ☐

Country Park/ Visitor Centre ☐

Bookshop ☐

Posters/leaflets (where from) ☐

....

Other (write in)

....
....
....
....
....

17. Are there any other comments you would like to make either about the route or the guidebook?

....

....

....

....

....

....

....

....

18. If you would like to receive more information about waymarked walks in Kent, please complete the following:

Name: Mr Mrs Ms ....

Address: ....

....

....

....

....

Post code ....

Thank you for your help, in return for which we will send you a voucher offering you a 10% discount against selected items from our wide range of countryside and coast products.

telephone Fairseat (01732) 823643.

Conservation Bodies

Medway River Project, 3 Lock Cottages, Lock Lane, Sandling, Maidstone, Kent ME17 3AU, telephone Maidstone (01622) 683695.

Kent Trust for Nature Conservation, Tyland Barn, Sandling, Maidstone, Kent ME14 3BD, telephone Maidstone (01622) 753017.

Countryside Commission, South East Regional Office, 4th Floor, 71 Kingsway, London WC2B 6ST, telephone (0171) 831 3510.

Miscellaneous

Ordnance Survey, Romsey Road, Maybush, Southampton, Hants SO9 4DH, telephone Southampton (01703) 792000.

Weatherdial (up-to-date weather forecast) Kent Area 0891 14 12 12

P & R Publicity Ltd (Achievement Badges for most long distance paths) Queensway, Stem Lane

Industrial Estate, New Milton, Hants BH25 5NN.

Accommodation

Bed and breakfast establishments are located in the following places: Tonbridge, Golden Green ($3/_4$ mile - 1.2 km), East Peckham ($1/_2$ mile - 0.8 km), Paddock Wood (2 miles - 3.2 km), Yalding Leas, Wateringbury ($1/_2$ mile - 0.8 km), Teston ($1/_3$ mile - 0.5 km), Maidstone, Allington ($1/_4$ mile - 0.4 km), Aylesford, Wouldham, Rochester. Please telephone the tourist information centres for details.

For a copy of the Kent Tourism Guide, contact Kent Tourism, Economic Development Department, Kent County Council, Springfield, Maidstone, Kent ME14 2LL, telephone Maidstone (01622) 696165.

The Ramblers' Association (also listed) publishes the Ramblers' Year Book and Accommodation Guide, which is available from local bookshops.

Medway Valley - A Story of its People and Places

Tonbridge - Hartlake Bridge

Tonbridge

Overlooking the Medway, Tonbridge Castle (1) (grid reference TQ 589466) was built to protect the river's crossing. The original Saxon fort was strengthened soon after the Norman Conquest, but was destroyed by fire in 1087. Such was the importance of the site that a replacement was immediately built on an artificial mound, or motte. The present sandstone gatehouse with its double drum towers dates from the 13th century, while the adjacent mansion housing the town's tourist information centre was built for domestic use at the end of the 18th century. When Horace Walpole came through in 1752 he was clearly impressed: 'The gateway is perfect,' he wrote, 'and the inclosure formed into a vineyard ... and the walls spread with fruit and the mount on which the keep stood planted in the same way.'

The town prospered when the Medway became navigable in the 1740s, thus enabling the transportation of locally grown fruit, hops and timber out to the estuary and along the Thames to London. Forty year later Tonbridge expanded as a communications centre with the advent of mail coaches, but it was the coming of the railway in the mid-19th century that fully underlined its importance, and at the same time began the decline of Medway navigation.

The river imposes its personality on town and countryside alike, and has created a serene and colourful heart to the commercial centre of Tonbridge. West of the castle, parks and open spaces offer a marked contrast to the crowded north-south development of the High Street, while the Medway's

behind the common yellow-starred ragwort has become a feature, while masses of the tall, pink-flowered policeman's helmet tower over the pathway. This member of the balsam family, a native of the Himalayas, has seed-bearing fruits that explode in the warmth. This is a particularly invasive plant that chokes out our native riverside plants; riverbanks become less diverse and therefore lose wildlife interest.

Between Cannon Bridge on the outskirts of town and Hartlake Bridge the towpath remains on the north bank of the river.

The Medway drains the heavy clay soils of the Low Weald by way of minor streams that flow from the Greensand hills in the north and from modest ridges in the south. As far as Hartlake Bridge (10) (grid reference TQ 629473) it edges a mixture of open meadow and arable farmland with brief strips of woodland, but then the orchards of Golden Green add a fresh dimension; in springtime trim rows of fruit trees are adorned with haloes of blossom.

Two hundred years ago historian Edward Hasted complained that this part of the Weald was 'too deep and mirey to be pleasant on account of the stiff clay soil.' But this 'stiff clay soil' bears excellent orchards and hop gardens, and students and staff of the Hadlow College of Agriculture (grid reference TQ 628498) put much of the land to productive good use.

illustration: ragged robin

asterly flow soon leads to ow-lying meadows and long ural views.

he walk begins and ends in Medway Wharf Road on the outh side of the Great ridge (2) (grid reference TQ 90465) which carries the igh Street across the river, he towpath being joined just before Town Lock, the first of ten such locks met between here and Allington, north of Maidstone.

Along this stretch of the river two particular wild flower species have colonised the bank with spectacular success. Even before urban development has been left

Hadlow Tower

The lofty eminence of Hadlow Tower (8) (grid reference TQ 635497) is a major landmark seen across the fields north of the river. Standing 170 feet high and dwarfing St Mary's Church next door, it was built by Walter Barton May as an addition to Hadlow Castle. Little remains of the castle today, but in 1823 it was described by Cobbett as: 'An immense house, stuck all over with a parcel of chimneys, or things like chimneys; little brick columns with a sort of cap at the top to catch the earwigs.' The tower is said to have been inspired by Beckford's Wiltshire folly, Fonthill, but there are two additional stories attached to it that are doubtless apocryphal. One suggests that May hoped to view the sea from the top; the other that he wished to keep an eye on his wife after she had left him and returned to her mother at Fish Hall $1^1/_2$ miles away.

Medway near Porters lock

Orange tip butterfly

2 Hartlake Bridge - Branbridges

At East Lock (grid reference TQ 642473) south of Golden Green the towpath transfers to the south bank and once again explores a combination of low meadow, woodland and arable fields. Oil seed rape is one of the more dominant crops grown here. In springtime a harsh blaze of yellow-gold adds a vibrancy to the chequerboard landscape, but with the coming of summer this colour dies as the crop collapses in a tangled mess to await the combine harvester.

Pillboxes

The only riverside buildings between the eastern limits of Tonbridge and industrial Branbridges are a few squat brick and concrete pillboxes remaining from the Second World War. Some are almost completely camouflaged by trees or brambles, while other stand clear as though ready to be used again. There have been calls to remove such constructions from the countryside, but there is a powerful argument in favour of their retention for, in common with medieval castles, these pillbox defences form a part of Britain's military heritage and stand as a constant reminder of the time when it was feared the river might provide an arterial route for invasion. It is interesting to speculate on how these simple defensive

Kingfisher

structures will be viewed by future historians and, indeed, by future generations of riverside ramblers. Will they be condemned as eyesores, or valued for their historic significance?

St Michael's Church

Near East Peckham a long view north shows beyond the village and its oast houses to a church on a ridge set among hop gardens and orchards (16) (grid reference TQ 662522). This is the abandoned church of St Michael's, formerly

Bluebells, Badsell Park Farm (MRP)

the parish church of East Peckham until the village moved a little over two miles south to exploit the river. From the churchyard a magnificent view is to be had southwards over the rich husbandry of the Medway valley.

Sluice Weir Lock (17) (grid reference TQ 670480) is the sixth from Tonbridge. A minor channel leaves the main course of the river and rejoins it downstream to the east of Branbridges. In 1812 an Act of Parliament was passed for the construction of a canal linking the

Medway at Branbridges with the Royal Military Canal at Appledore on the edge of Romney Marsh. However, the project was deemed financially unviable and was never begun.

Whitbread Hop Farm

South of the river is the Whitbread Hop Farm (18) (grid reference TQ 675474) well-known for its massed oast houses - the largest collection in the world. The farm began in 1836 and was bought by Whitbread the brewers in 1920, who then

developed it as one of the Kent's largest hop farms. It has since become a major tourist attraction.

The Whitbread oasts are Victorian, with rounded kilns. Elsewhere (near Twyford Bridge at Yalding, for example), one may notice the square-built oasts in which hops were traditionally dried. As a general rule square oasts date from the 18th century, while the rounded versions were built in the 19th century.

Banded damoisoille

3 Branbridges - Nettlestead Church

Banbridges to Twyford Bridge

There is a world of difference between the area of small industrial units at Branbridges and the holiday atmosphere of Twyford Bridge outside Yalding. One is drab and grey, the other bright and cheerful; one workmanlike and indifferent to its surroundings, the other relaxed and informal and, at times, almost hysterically jovial.

The countryside linking the two shows similar contrasts; seemingly unloved in places, but tended and cared-for elsewhere. Walking from one to the other is to experience a crowded, tangled exuberance of vegetation as well as open aspects of broad meadow and long views to hillsides patterned with acres of

orchard and fruit bush. Giant hogweed towers over the path, each parasol head massed with tiny flowers - beware, its sap is a powerful irritant to exposed skin. Butterflies drift among bright yellow clumps of ragwort and tansy, and transport themselves with seeming indecision to straggling wands of buddleia whose pyramids of bloom add fresh colour along the towpath.

The towpath is sometimes forced away from the riverbank by this over-abundance of growth; it would not always have been so. Try to plot the development of riverside plants as you walk and ask yourself what changes have taken place since the early days of the Medway's navigation.

Among the many riverside trees, alder, ash, oak, chestnut and willow are full of birdsong in late spring. Look for kestrels hovering overhead and keep alert also to the

Adder

possibility of sighting the brilliant flash of a kingfisher - elusive but by no means rare along the Medway.

Going downstream to Twyford Bridge the towpath remains on the right (south-east) bank which, after passing beneath an ugly

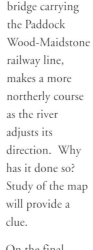

Comfrey, arrowhead and yellow waterlilly

bridge carrying the Paddock Wood-Maidstone railway line, makes a more northerly course as the river adjusts its direction. Why has it done so? Study of the map will provide a clue.

On the final approach to Twyford Bridge a view opens to fertile hills described by Cobbett as ' ... the best finest, as to fertility and diminutive beauty, in the whole world ... There are, on rising ground, not only hop gardens and beautiful woods, but immense orchards of apples, pears, plums, cherries, filberts, and these, in many cases, with gooseberries and currants and raspberries beneath.'

On the western bank of the river stand the four, square-built Parsonage oasts; on

the opposite bank a boatyard, with the River Teise (21) flowing in to join the Medway.

Yalding

Yalding (22) boasts two medieval bridges, Twyford Bridge (23) (grid reference TQ 691498), with its sharp pointed cutwaters, is one of the finest on the Medway. Built around 1325, part of it collapsed in 1939 and a brick parapet was added in 1980. The other spans the River Beult with seven arches, and is found a half mile to the north-east. More narrow and, at 100 feet, much longer

than Twyford Bridge, Town Bridge (grid reference TQ 698500) leads directly into the main street, a handsome, unselfconscious place lined with a delightful mixture of buildings. A cluster of oasts stands behind the 17th-century ragstone Church of St Peter and St Paul with its curious onion dome on top of the tower (grid reference TQ 699501).

The longest of the Medway tributaries, the River Beult, joins just west of Yalding among low-lying meadows of The Lees. All this area used to suffer regular flooding by the three rivers, but flow-gauging stations and the Flood Relief Barrier above Tonbridge have helped reduce the danger during heavy rainfall.

Twyford Bridge to Nettlestead

The river forks at Twyford Bridge. Its natural course flows beneath the bridge and makes a gentle arc through water meadows to be joined by the Beult, before veering north below Nettlestead Green. However, a short canal section has been created beside the Anchor Inn to direct river craft alongside Hampstead Lane to the deepest of its locks before curving north to rejoin the main arm of the river once more. Hop gardens line Hampstead Lane. At its northern end the towpath is rejoined below Hampstead Lock (grid reference TQ 686503) and briefly shares the route of the Greensand Way (24). Between here and Teston Lock and beyond to Maidstone the towpath remains on the west bank, although the main route

follows the opposite bank between Bow Bridge and Teston Bridge.

South of Wateringbury the riverbank develops into an overgrown jungle of nettles, ragwort, tansy, rosebay willowherb and giant hogweed in summer, much to the benefit of butterflies and other insects.

Roydon Hall

North-west of Nettlestead Green, but unseen from the towpath, stands Roydon Hall (25) (grid reference TQ 666517), a step-gabled house dating from the 16th century. At the time of the Civil War it was owned by Sir Roger Twysden, a Royalist pamphleteer, and 200 years after the war ended an informative diary of those momentous times was discovered in the cellars. In 1947 it became a centre for the international transcendental meditation movement.

Mereworth Castle

Above the western bank the ground rises beyond the railway. Hidden from view one and a half miles away, Mereworth Castle (26) (grid reference TQ 668534) is an extravagant 18th-century Palladian villa built by Colen Campbell for the Hon John Fane, later Earl of Westmoreland. Deciding that Mereworth village spoiled his view, he built a new village out of sight to the

St Mary's Church. Nettlestead

Cobb Platt, Nettlestead (MRP)

the door - remnants of a number of stained glass windows erected by Reginald de Pympe in the 15th century and destroyed by hailstones in a storm on 19 August 1763.

In the river below the church a small island gives rise to speculation that there was a crossing place here either in the Iron Age (there was an Iron Age camp at Nettlestead) or during the Roman occupation.

west and pulled the original houses down.

Nettlestead

Medieval Nettlestead Place (27) (grid reference TQ 685520) appears among trees on the west bank, and it is worth making a short diversion to visit the church next door. A narrow path climbs from the river, crosses the railway and enters the churchyard through a crumbling archway. St Mary's (28) (grid reference TQ 685521) has a 13th-century tower, 15th-century nave, and a jigsaw puzzle of 500-year-old fragments of glass in the window opposite

4 Nettlestead Church - Barming Church

Wateringbury

Below Wateringbury (29) the river is lined with pleasure craft and a string of caravans on the bank with trim little gardens around them. The village itself, whose name means 'fortress by the river', spreads east from the area called Pizien Well with a few charming old houses. The church contains a unique curiosity in an ancient manorial staff of office, the Dumb Borsholder of Chart; this 36 inch truncheon-like oak stick fitted with metal rings and an iron spike was used for breaking down the doors of offenders. The last holder of the office was village blacksmith Thomas Clampard, who died in 1748.

Parish Clerk Edward Greensted left a personal record of the great storm that swept the Medway valley in August 1763. So severe was it that hailstones measuring ten inches in diameter battered crops, trees and buildings. Some of the hailstones remained in heaps for more than a month, while others were sent to London to be exhibited as curiosities.

Waregrave's Wood

The main route follows the south bank of the Medway between Bow Bridge and Teston Bridge, passing through the lower edge of Waregrave's Wood (30) (grid reference TQ 699527). The woodland has been here at least since medieval times and is important for the coppicing that has been practised in it. Coppicing is a traditional method of harvesting woodland by felling trees and allowing them to shoot again from a stump. Shoots grow in a thick cluster and, depending on use, can be harvested again after seven to 20 years. In the past, Wealden woods were coppiced for iron-smelting, but in more recent times the main use has been for fencing, tool-making or the provision of hop poles. Sweet chestnut, hazel and, in some instances, hornbeam may be grown specifically for their multi-harvest value, but in the case of Waregrave's Wood approximately one hectare (two and a half acres) of ash trees is being coppiced. Apart from fencing, tool-

Green woodpecker

making and hop poles, coppiced timber has a number of other traditional uses; can you list a few of them? Coppicing also benefits wildlife - do you know why? On the eastern side there is a fine view, looking down from the hillside to a twist of river, while from River Mill Cottages, Teston Lock and weir may be seen below.

Above Waregrave's Wood, to the north of a barn near Tutsham Hall, stands a row of trees

Medway between Wateringbury and Teston Lock

whose leaves whose fruit appear at first glance like those of the chestnut. Do you know what these trees are - and the uses to which their fruit is put?

Teston

Teston was home to one of the knights who murdered Thomas à Becket in Canterbury Cathedral in 1170. After he fled to Ireland his land passed into the ownership of Robert de Berham, whose name lives on in Barham Court (31), the large house seen above

sweeping lawns on the edge of the village (grid reference TQ 707537). In the 18th century Edward Hasted considered it the greatest ornament in this part of Kent, while William Wilberforce, a frequent visitor, wrote that 'for charm of softness and elegance I never beheld a superior to Barham Court'. Its view of the river must be quite splendid, for the medieval bridge (32) (grid reference TQ 709533) that spans the Medway makes a lovely scenic feature.

Teston Lock (grid reference TQ 709530) was constructed in about 1740 by the Medway Navigation

Company, and rebuilt from 1911-19. On the eastern bank nearby can be seen the remains of an old mill, green with age and hung about with ivy. To the north and west of the lock Teston Picnic Site (34) covers some 30 acres of riverside meadows.

The river draws visitors to its banks for many different reasons, and the picnic site concentrates large numbers in a comparatively small area. What recreational uses does the Medway have, and what are the associated effects on both plantlife and wildlife?

Writing in 1823 William Cobbett expressed his obvious pleasure in the farmland between Maidstone and Mereworth. He called it ' ... the finest ... I have ever seen in England or anywhere else ... I should think there were hop-gardens on one half of the way on both sides of the road. Then, looking across the Medway, you see hop-gardens and orchards two miles deep, on the side of a gently rising ground.'

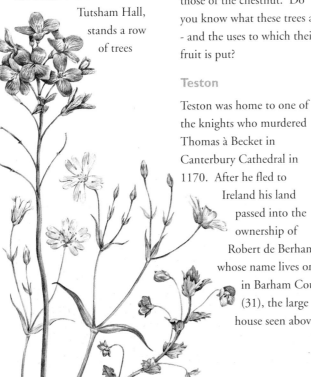
Speedwell, stitchwort and cuckoo flower

Hop gardens and orchards are still a feature, though less so than in Cobbett's day. Maidstone has spread its tentacles, villages have grown and a combination of various factors, including increased competition from foreign growers, has brought about a decline in the English hop industry. Yet for those who follow the Medway towpath the stately poles and cat's-cradles of wires that adorn acres of 'gently rising ground' continue to form an integral part of the scene.

Downstream from Teston Bridge open meadows drain to the river; a very popular area with anglers and families enjoying summer picnics. Sprouting from the very water's edge tough stems of water mint grow unchecked, their leaves giving off a strong fragrance of peppermint when crushed, while another member of the mint family enjoying the same habitat is the gipsywort, with nettle-like leaves and whitish flowers.

Willow warbler

In anglers' keep-nets you may see roach, chub and perch. What other fish are to be found in the Medway?

West Farleigh

Above the eastern bank, and reached by footpath from the east end of the bridge, stands an early Norman church (grid reference TQ 715535), somewhat divorced from the main part of the parish it was built to serve. Except for the tower and vestry, most of All Saints Church, West Farleigh (35) dates from about 1100, and is thought to have been built by Robert de Crevecoeur, the man responsible for Leeds Castle. Next door are the farm buildings of Court Lodge.

Barming

A major landmark downstream of Teston Bridge is the elegant shingled spire of St Margaret's Church, Barming (36) (grid reference TQ 720542). At the time of the Domesday survey, Barming was divided between east (nearest the church) and west; the latter part, also known as Little Barming, had its own church until the end of the 15th century.

Ruined mill near Teston Lock

5 Barming Church - Maidstone

East Barming

Below East Barming the river is spanned by Kettle Bridge (37) (grid reference TQ 724538), sometimes known as Barming or St Helen's Bridge, which leads to the hamlet of Kettle Corner via St Helen's Lane. This is the only timber-built vehicular bridge on the Medway, and although it is safe for cars to use, it was apparently not strong enough in 1914 to take a traction engine which, with its crew of four, broke through and landed in the river.

The railway maintains close company with the towpath between East Barming and Maidstone, but the sound of trains rarely intrudes upon the peaceful nature of the walk. The river is well-shaded and the towpath dodges among the shrubs and beneath trees. There comes one particular point where a lovely view is had along an avenue of water, leaf and reed to East Farleigh Church.

Bur-reed and water lily threaten the shallows with their prodigious growth. Dragonflies and damselflies hover over the water, then dart in staccato bursts to and fro with the sunlight flashing on transparent wings. Study their flight and see if you can discover what it is they feed upon.

East Farleigh

A caravan site lies between railway and river, and the Medway itself is bright with moored craft west of the splendid medieval bridge (28) (grid reference TQ 735536) that is one of the highlights of East Farleigh (39). During the Civil War, General Fairfax and his men came over this bridge on their way to engage in battle with Royalist forces in Maidstone. At its northern end is a 19th-century waterworks building; on the south side an old hoppers' hut; above it on the hill the parish church has a view of the valley and a clutch of oast houses nearby. The churchyard contains a simple wooden cross erected over the grave of 'forty three strangers who died of cholera' in 1849,

Honey bees

and the grave too of writer and artist Donald Maxwell, whose books illustrate many of the county's odd corners.

East Farleigh was already established at the time of the Domesday Book. Then it consisted of 'a church, three mills, six eel fisheries, 12 acres of pastures and wood for 115 hogs.' Long before that a Roman nobleman had a villa here, the remains of which were discovered when William Wilberforce's son was the incumbent at the church.

Loose

A little under two miles south-east of the river, tucked in a steep valley, lies the village of Loose (40) (grid reference TQ 756521), a charming, secretive place of ponds, running water and delightful causeways. Its stream, flowing between Langley and the Medway at Tovil, once powered 13 mills, while local quarries supplied much-needed ragstone. Spanning the valley above the village is a lofty viaduct designed by Thomas Telford and erected in 1829 to facilitate the movement of troops during the Napoleonic Wars. The half-timbered Wool House near the church is thought to have served as either a fulling mill or fleece store. It is now a private house owned by the National Trust and open to view on written request.

Maidstone

Approached along the towpath, Maidstone comes as a surprise. Much of the suburb of Tovil (41) on the south eastern bank is hidden, so almost the first indication one has that the county town is near is the sight of the elegant ragstone Church of All Saints (42) (grid reference TQ 760554) rising among trees on a curve of the river. Next to it on one side is the medieval College of Priests (43), and on the other the former Archbishop's Palace (44) (grid reference TQ 759554). This lovely group, with the Medway as a foreground, presents an attractive and welcoming sight and makes the best possible entrance to the town from the south.

Maidstone has a chequered history. The Domesday survey lists six mills, a church and two salt houses. By the Middle Ages it had grown as an industrial and agricultural centre with the Medway being the main means of transportation of goods to outside markets. Locally quarried ragstone, sand and fullers earth were shipped downstream by barge. Later, papermaking and brewing became important to the town's prosperity. But led by Thomas Wyatt, Maidstone

Dogs mercury, yellow archangel and bluebells

Strangers Cross, East Farleigh

backed the 1554 rebellion against Queen Mary and was subsequently stripped of its charter of incorporation. Maidstone lost its charter and Wyatt lost his head. However, the charter was restored five years later by Elizabeth I and the town became a borough '... enabled to have voice in Parleament'. Not only was Maidstone able to elect two members to Parliament, but authorisation was once more given to hold a weekly market and a fair four times a year. The right to a market had first been granted by Henry III in 1261, and since that right was reinstated in 1559 one has been held regularly for more than 400 years.

The best of Maidstone is found to the east of the Medway. Rising from the bridge (45) (grid reference TQ 758555) over the river, the High Street gradually widens and forks to create an island occupied by the Town Hall (46) (grid reference TQ 759556). Bank Street runs alongside it lined by a number of 17th-century buildings, but immediately before coming to this Mill Street breaks away to the right. Along here are the Archbishop's Stables (47) and on the other side of the road a small rectangular 14th-century gatehouse (48) (grid reference TQ 759555) with a section of medieval bridge spanning the River Len, one of the tributaries of the Medway.

South of the gatehouse is the Archbishop's Palace, built for Archbishop Islip in 1348 using stone brought from the dismantled palace at Wrotham. Internally there are huge beams and heavy panelling, and in the riverside dungeons John Ball, the 'Mad Priest of Kent', was

imprisoned for preaching social revolution. The Palace is now in the hands of the town council.

All Saints Church is huge. Generally considered the finest of the county's Perpendicular churches, it was built in 1395 as a collegiate church by Archbishop Courtenay on the site of a Saxon place of worship. In it Fairfax held 1300 Royalist prisoners in the Civil War. In 1730 it lost its spire when struck by lightning. The College of Priests nearby was also founded by Courtenay for a master and 24 chaplains and clerks. The Master's House is now

home to the Kent Music School, while the tall, battlemented gatehouse facing the church is the most impressive part of the college.

Maidstone - Aylesford Friary

Each July, Maidstone celebrates with a River Festival, but throughout the summer the Medway is bright with boats and bunting as assorted craft are moored in close formation north of the Archbishop's Palace, while the Kentish Lady II makes a familiar sight as she cruises to and from the Malta Inn at Allington Lock, providing a short but colourful journey along the river.

Throughout its length the River Medway suffers pollution from a wide variety of sources; some are natural, but others occur through man's ignorance or indifference. Consider some of the causes of river pollution and how they can be reduced.

All the way to Rochester now the riverside walk keeps to the east bank. Near St Peter's Bridge (grid reference TQ 756555) is the site of the old town wharf where barges laden with sand, ragstone and fullers earth used to set off for London. For a while the unlovely clutter of industrial Maidstone creates a stark contrast to the mellow grace of church, college and palace that so elegantly adorned the east bank upstream. But for all its drab appearance, the downstream quarter of the county town soon slips back to more harmonious scenes - down by the river, at least. For the Medway once more injects an atmosphere of hinted rural calm far removed from the strident tones which inevitably accompany areas of commerce and industry.

Penenden Heath

On the northern edge of town, Penenden Heath (54)

(grid reference TQ 771575) marks the place where England's first recorded trial was held in 1076 between Archbishop Lanfranc and Bishop Odo of Bayeux. This ancient meeting place was later used for public executions and the burning of witches but is now a recreation ground.

Harts tongue fern and ivy leaf toadflax

Allington Castle

The Medway writhes its way downstream and on a bend on the west bank is seen a small portion of Tennyson's 'Castle Adamant' - Allington Castle (57) (grid reference TQ 753579), whose original battlements were added in 1281 by Stephen de Penchester in order to fortify his manor house. Two hundred years later the castle was bought by Sir Henry Wyatt who added a Tudor range with a long gallery.

The Wyatts of Allington lived in dangerous times. Sir Henry was imprisoned in the Tower of London by Richard III where, it is said, he was saved from starvation by a cat that brought a pigeon to his cell each morning. Today brown pigeons fly about the castle walls as if to keep the legend alive.

Henry's son, Sir Thomas, was the man who introduced the sonnet to England and the poet who loved Anne Boleyn. She was a frequent visitor to Allington, as were Henry VIII, Thomas Cromwell and

Cardinal Wolsey. Sir Thomas had a son who also became Sir Thomas, a tragic figure who led the Kentish revolt against Queen Mary and lost his head for his troubles. With his demise Allington Castle fell to neglect and when Lord Conway bought it for £4,800 in 1905 it was virtually a ruin. Conway spent £70,000 on the castle's restoration, and in 1951 it was sold by his daughter to the Carmelite Friars as a religious retreat.

On the lane leading to the castle, the shingle-spired Church of St Lawrence (58) (grid reference TQ 748578), rebuilt in the 19th century only to become redundant 100 years later, has been converted to a private house.

Allington Lock

Below Allington Castle the river makes a determined curve westward, with a string of traditional barges moored along the right bank leading to the Malta Inn, where a 'river bus' operates a regular summer service to Maidstone. Just beyond the

inn is Allington Lock (59) (grid reference TQ 747582), the first and last of the ten locks of the Medway navigation. Below this point the river is tidal, but if the gates were to be left open the tidal flow would extend another four miles upstream. The flood barrier (60) next to the lock controls water levels by means of electrically operated automatic sluices.

Allington Quarry

A short distance away from the river on the western bank is Allington Quarry (61) (grid reference TQ 738578). For centuries ragstone has been quarried from the Medway valley, for Kentish

Rag has long been a popular building material and until the reign of Henry VIII it was also used for moulding into cannon-balls.

Over a period of about ten million years, deposits of calcareous materials settled on the rocks which had formed the Wealden bed some 140 million years ago. These deposits became known as the Hythe Beds (part of the Lower Greensand series), with the escarpment being lifted as its most prominent feature between the downs and the Low Weald. From the Lower Greensand, a hard core of ragstone has been exposed by erosion and

Fern and fungi

subsequently exploited for its obvious qualities in construction work. Many of Kent's most attractive buildings owe their mellow glory to the weathering of this local stone.

Museum of Kent Rural Life

On the right bank of the river a 27-acre site portrays rural life in Kent from the late 18th to the early-20th centuries. In addition to livestock, hop garden, orchards, kitchen and herb gardens, the story of hop growing is displayed, in an oast house, and there are huts in which hop-pickers from London lived during their annual working holidays. The museum (62) (grid reference TQ 748583) holds frequent craft demonstrations and occasional special events include ploughing and hop-picking.

Remains of gateway, Boxley Abbey

Boxley Abbey

About three-quarters of a mile north-east of Allington Lock, and standing on private land, are the remains of Boxley Abbey (63) (grid reference TQ 761587). Founded by William of Ypres in 1146, this Cistercian abbey became infamous in the Middle Ages for an elaborate hoax played by monks to gain money from pious pilgrims by manipulating two statues, one the Rood of Grace, the other of the improbable infant Saint Rumwold. The Rood (a 'miracle-working' figure of Christ on the Cross)

was publicly burned in 1539, the year after Boxley had been dissolved.

All that remain are creeper-covered perimeter walls and a wide, incomplete entrance arch, but Boxley Abbey Barn (64) survives. A magnificent structure, this ragstone tithe barn was built around the 13th century and, measuring 186 feet in length, is still in regular use.

A short distance from Boxley Abbey, Tyland Barn (65) (grid reference TQ 754594) houses the headquarters of the Kent Trust for Nature Conservation. In the visitor centre there are displays of all the county's major habitats.

Allington to Aylesford

The river has a voice all its own. Above Allington Lock it has its soft lapping sounds, gentle at times but expressed with vigour with the wash of a passing boat; rushing and urgent at a weir or when a lock is being filled, calmly subdued elsewhere as it idles towards the sea. Below Allington Lock the river is tidal, and when the tide is out black mud exposed to the air begins to bubble and seethe. Low sucking sounds are heard; strange voices that gurgle, belch and swallow. And then the gulls and common terns come paddling, prodding and prying in the shallows. When the tide is in they swoop and dive, the terns especially prodigious in their aerobatic displays.

The river's vegetation is affected by the tides. Can you see what differences there are in plants growing upstream of Allington Lock, and those of the tidal downstream region? Can you see any difference in the wildlife species attracted to the river?

In 1669 Samuel Pepys journeyed to Aylesford and '... had the pleasure of seeing the Medway running, winding up and down mightily, and a very fine country'.

Industry dominates the Medway between Aylesford and Rochester. Papermills and cement factories hug the western bank while quarries and sandpits pock the valley and hillsides. Through the Medway gap march lines of silver skeletons - pylons carrying electricity cables.

Aylesford

For such an attractive and historic place, Aylesford (66) suffers the double indignity of being choked by traffic and ambushed by a conglomeration of warehouses and factories. Its saviour is its history, for it claims to be England's oldest continuously occupied village. Settled in Neolithic times, the site was chosen because the river was easily fordable at low tide. This ford also attracted the Romans, and in 455 AD Hengist and Horsa led their Saxon warriors in battle against Vortigern and his native Britons.

The view of Aylesford tightly packed across the river, with the graceful five-arched ragstone bridge in the foreground, makes a classic composition. The bridge (67) (grid reference TQ 729589) was built in 1390 to replace a wooden structure,

but three piers were removed in 1824 and the central arch subsequently enlarged to ease the passage of boats heading upriver to Maidstone.

The Church of St Peter and St Paul (68) (grid reference TQ 729590) stands head and shoulders above the village, with its sturdy square tower rising from a Norman base containing pieces of Roman tile. Inside the north chancel contains memorials to Sir Thomas Culpeper and Pepys' business acquaintance Sir John Banks, who lived at The Friars (see below).

Below the church and set beside a brook-bordered greensward on the Rochester Road is a lovely row of gabled almshouses (60) (grid reference TQ 732591) erected in 1605 and restored in 1842.

The Friars

When the Carmelites came to England in 1241, they were granted a small piece of land on which they built a modest chapel. By the time of the Reformation their land had

The Friars, Aylesford

extended to 18 acres and The Friars (70) (grid reference TQ 723589) consisted of a number of buildings, but the monks were dispossessed of their property which then passed into the hands of the Wyatts of Allington Castle. Later, in the 17th century, Sir John Banks lived there.

During his day Pepys visited and wrote that 'he keeps the grounds about it, and walls and house, very handsome.'

In 1949 the Carmelites returned to the riverbank site which had first been theirs 700 years earlier. Today The Friars is a splendid place of peace and openness whose buildings reflect a variety of architectural styles. Open daily to the public, there is a conference centre, and accommodation for visitors in the guest house.

Aylesford Friary - Old Church Road

Sand and Gravel Pits

North of Aylesford lies an extensive area of sand and gravel pits, some of which have flooded and been adopted by a variety of wildfowl. Peering into one of these (grid reference TQ 727595) from the path between Aylesford and Eccles, try to work out how the sand was first laid down, and then see how many different species of bird you can identify on projections of land within the flooded area.

Eccles

Surrounded by low-lying farmland and quarries, the site of the village was occupied during Roman times, for the remains of an elaborate villa were discovered here. Eccles (71) enjoyed a brief spell of expansion in the mid-19th century when a number of homes were built to house workers for the brick and cement works then being developed along the valley.

Why was the cement industry attracted to the Medway valley?

Kit's Coty House

About one mile east of Eccles and set high on the North Downs is one of Kent's oldest man-made structures. Kit's Coty House (72) (grid reference TQ 745608) is the remains of a Neolithic burial chamber some 5,000 years old - three upright stones with a mighty capstone still resting on them. In the 18th century the covering barrow was said to be almost 200 feet long, but this has since disappeared.

In a field below lies the jumble of half-buried sarsen stones known as Little Kit's Coty (73) (grid reference TQ 744604), the remains of another Neolithic tomb whose original chamber was demolished in 1690, while a short distance to the east stands the White Horse Stone (74) (grid reference TQ 752602). This large block hidden among trees is a dolmen marking the site of a megalithic tomb. One needs a vivid imagination, however, to see any likeness to a horse, white or otherwise, in this secluded piece of ancient history.

Goldfinches

North Downs

The chalk-ribbed upland of the North Downs (75) forms a natural boundary to the Weald and a complementary calliper to that of the South Downs. At one time the Weald was covered by a great dome of chalk produced by an accumulation of minuscule shell-bearing organisms that had settled on the bed of a shallow sea, the pure calcium carbonate of their shells powdering to a dust that accumulated at a rate of just one foot every 30,000 years or so. In due course this chalk attained a depth of around 1,000 feet, was buckled and raised above the sea, and then became exposed to forces of erosion. The dome that covered the Weald has been washed away now, and only the North and South Downs remain to illustrate the extent of that marvellous act of patience and persistence which is the hallmark of the natural world.

From very early times the North Downs escarpment formed a natural route for continental immigrants travelling through southern England. Why, do you think, was this so?

On the route, several acres of woodland and scrub, bright with golden rod, rosebay willowherb, tansy and ragwort, elder and rich-fruiting bramble, create an effective camouflage to the sewage works and wastepaper yards that otherwise offend the eye between Eccles and the river.

Snodland

Across the river at Snodland, Brooklands Lake (77) (grid reference TQ 710613) provides a watersports amenity with fishing, canoeing, sailing and windsurfing being enjoyed there. Snodland was formerly noted as a crossing place, and for hundreds of years a ferry made the short journey across to Burham. Very much an agricultural community until the 19th century, it is an ugly place today, dominated by a massive papermill.

Burham

With the coming of the cement industry to the Medway valley, Burham (78) moved away from the river and in 50 years virtually quadrupled its population, leaving its church (79) (grid reference TQ 717620) stranded near Burham Court. On land nearby evidence of a Roman villa has

Pipestrelle bats

been discovered, while close to the Medway's bank more Roman remains have been exposed. Burham village itself lines the route of the Pilgrims' Way (80) near abandoned chalkpits. The name of Little Culand to the south is a reminder of Great Culland House which stood for nearly 400 years until being demolished in 1953. The wooden treadmill that used to draw water from its well is now displayed outside Maidstone museum.

Horseshoe Reach

On the Medway a raised embankment round Horseshoe Reach (81) creates a walk of little over a mile and brushes against a frieze of reedbeds that all but hides the river itself. This is part of a nature reserve managed by the Kent Trust for Nature Conservation.

Horseshoe Reach is aptly named. Why? What will happen to the river at this point unless man interferes with its natural course?

8 Old Church Road - Nashenden Farm

Wouldham

Wouldham is a long ribbon of village linked by ferry with Halling until 1963. Walter Burke, Nelson's purser aboard the 'Victory' who cradled the dying admiral in his arms, is buried in the churchyard (82) (grid reference TQ 713644) where each Trafalgar Day local children place flowers on his grave. Bordering Wouldham Marshes, the river curves north-eastward to break through the downs, and a path treads an embankment alongside it. Watch for herons in the water course and damp meadows inland.

Starkey Castle Farm

Starkey Castle Farm (83) (grid reference TQ 714656) is a fine ragstone building being lovingly restored. Designated a monument of national importance, the moated manor house was built for Sir Humphrey Starkey in the 15th century.

From the hillside above nearby Ivy Cottage (grid reference TQ 726650) it is possible to survey a large extent of the lower Medway valley with the North Downs curving into the blue distance out to the south-west. Imagine how that valley must have looked before the downs were breached by the river.

Lapwing

9 Nashenden Farm - Rochester

M2 Bridge

Between Wouldham Marshes and Rochester the river is magnificently spanned by the towering concrete edifice of the M2 motorway bridge (84) (grid reference TQ 724670) which not only carries motor traffic but also has a walkway used by the North Downs Way.

Baty's Marsh

Baty's Marsh (85) is a prominent site whether viewed downstream from Rochester city centre, or from the North Downs Way, which runs across the M2 motorway bridge. It affords excellent views over the Medway Estuary.

It consists of typical saltmarsh, intersected by winding channels which fill at high tide. There is also a

small but significant area of mud which is exposed at low tide. The marsh is backed by a narrow belt of scrub and predominantly rough grassland. Various species of bird visit the saltmarsh in winter, and breed in the scrub during the summer months.

Rochester

On the city side of the motorway bridge, the saltings of Baty's Marsh (85) near the marina form part of a Local Nature Reserve (LNR) on the very edge of industrial Rochester. Industry in turn gives way to the residential

waterfront which, with its modern development, surprisingly complements the noble keep of the castle (86) (grid reference TQ 741686) that enjoys such a grandstand view of both river and city.

The importance of the site was obvious to Belgic tribes long before the Romans settled there around 43 AD along the route of Watling Street, the Dover to

London road. The walls of the Roman town, called Durobrivae (meaning 'stronghold by the bridge'), encompassed 23$\frac{1}{2}$ acres, and their line can be traced today in the High Street where sections of medieval wall, built upon the original, are clearly visible. When the Saxons came they merely added to Roman defences and erected a timber bridge across the Medway, replacing the Roman one of timber and stone more or less where the modern Rochester Bridge (87) (grid reference TQ 741689) stands.

Britain's second-oldest cathedral (88) (grid reference TQ 743685) was built on the site of an earlier Saxon church founded by Bishop Justus in 604 AD. Over a period of some 400 years the early church withstood numerous raids by the Vikings, resulting in a fleet of ships being built there and England's first navy being formed by King Alfred. In 1080 the great Norman architect, Bishop Gundulph, began construction of the

High tide on the Medway

cathedral and just seven years later turned his skills to creating one of England's earliest masonry castles on the hill, once fortified by the Romans, overlooking the Medway. The dimensions are impressive. It stands 113 feet high, is 70 feet square and has walls between 11 and 13 feet thick. When King John lay siege to the castle for two months in 1215, he finally gained entry by undermining the keep and using the fat from forty pigs to set fire to

pit props under the south-west tower.

Guarding both the Medway and the important trunk road of Watling Street, it is hardly surprising that Rochester should be such an historic place. During the Middle Ages both pilgrims and crusaders passed through on their way to the Holy Land. One such was a baker from Perth in Scotland, named William, who was murdered just outside the city in 1201

and buried in the cathedral. Canonised as a saint, his tomb was venerated as it was believed to possess miraculous healing powers. The tomb was destroyed in 1538. At Strood, on the north bank of the river, Knights Templar on their way to the Crusades found lodgings in the 13th-century Temple Manor built specifically for that purpose.

The river has always played a major part in the very

Rochester Castle

Chatham (Sir Francis Drake learned to sail on the Medway), while some 400 Royal Navy ships including Nelson's HMS Victory, were built there over a period of four centuries.

But for all its history, Rochester leans heavily on the writings and personality of Charles Dickens, who spent much of his life in and around the city and wove many of its buildings into his novels. A Dickens Festival is held there each summer; there is a Charles Dickens Centre and a city trail which picks out the most interesting features of Dickens' Rochester - the Medway town with two thousand years of history.

existence of Rochester and its neighbouring towns. In 1078 Bishop Gundulph founded a hospital in what is now Chatham (St Bartholomew's Chapel is said to be part of Gundulph's original hospital), while the Sir John Hawkins Hospital opposite was founded for 'poor decayed mariners and shipwrights' by the famed Elizabethan navigator. In 1547 Henry VIII's fleet was serviced at the tiny dockyard, and in 1588 many of the ships that defeated the Spanish Armada sailed from

Sedge warbler

Reed warbler

Medway Valley - Exploring the Area

Interesting places to visit

on or near the Medway Valley Walk

Tonbridge Castle
High Street, Tonbridge
Tel: (01732) 770929

Caxton Tonbridge Waterways
Tonbridge Castle grounds, Tonbridge
Tel: (01732) 360630

Whitbread Hop Farm
Beltring, Paddock Wood
Tel: (01622) 872068

Wool House (National Trust (NT)
Wells Street, Loose, Maidstone
Tel: (01892) 890651

Stoneacre (NT)
Otham, Maidstone
Tel: (01622) 862871

Archbishops Palace and Heritage Centre
Mill Street, Maidstone
Tel: (01622) 663006

Tyrwhitt-Drake Museum of Carriages
Archbishops Stables, Mill Street, Maidstone
Tel: (01622) 754497

Medway River Cruises
Undercliffe Boathouse, Bishops Way, Maidstone
Tel: (01622) 753740

Maidstone Town Hall
High Street, Maidstone
Tel: (01622) 602164

Maidstone Museum and Art Gallery
Chillington Manor House, St Faith's Street, Maidstone
Tel: (01622) 663006

Kent Museum of Rural Life
Lock Lane, Sandling, Maidstone
Tel: (01622) 763936

Tyland Barn Wildlife Visitor Centre
Kent Trust for Nature Conservation, Sandling, Maidstone
Tel: (01622) 662012

The Friars
Aylesford
Tel: (01622) 717272

Kit's Coty House (English Heritage (EH)
Bluebell Hill, near Maidstone
Tel: (01732) 778000

Rochester Castle (EH)
Rochester
Tel: (01634) 402276

Rochester Cathedral
Rochester
Tel: (01634) 843366

Guildhall Museum
High Street, Rochester
Tel: (01634) 848717

Watts Charity
High Street, Rochester
Tel: (01634) 845609

Charles Dickens Centre
Eastgate House, High Street,
Rochester
Tel: (01634) 844176

Parish Churches - en route
(key usually obtained locally,
if not open)

Lamp-post on Great Bridge, Tonbridge

Countryside open spaces

on or near the Medway
Valley Walk

Haysden Country Park
Lower Haysden Lane,
Tonbridge
Tel: (01732) 844522

Teston Bridge Picnic Site
Teston
Tel: (01622) 817623

Mote Park
Mote Avenue, Maidstone
Tel: (01622) 602188

Brenchley Gardens
Behind Chillington Manor,
St Faith's Street, Maidstone

Cobtree Manor Park
Forstal Road, Sandling,
Maidstone
Tel: (01622) 602188

Bluebell Hill Picnic Site
Bluebell Hill, near Maidstone
Tel: (01474) 823800

Brookland Lake
Snodland
Tel: (01634) 240228

Baty's Marsh Nature
Reserve
Borstal, Rochester

Other Walking opportunities

If you have enjoyed this walk
and would like to explore
other waymarked walking
routes in Kent, write to the
Access and Recreation Officer
(listed elsewhere) for an
information pack.

In series with 'Medway Valley
Walk' are the 'Greensand
Way', 'Stour Valley Walk',
'Elham Valley Way', 'High
Weald Walk' and 'Eden
Valley Walk'. Other route
guidebooks are planned and
in preparation.

Copies of these or any other
walking guides can be
obtained from bookshops,
libraries, tourist information
centres and the Access and
Recreation Officer.

It is possible to devise your
own shorter linear and
circular walks using the
extensive rights of way
network throughout the
county. Details about these
can be obtained by studying
either the Ordnance Survey
Pathfinder maps or the
County Council Definitive
Maps of Public Rights of

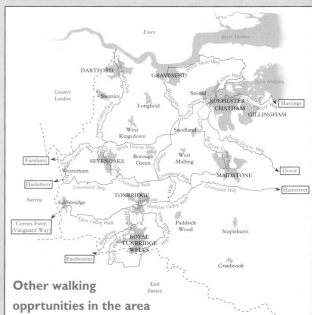

Other walking opprtunities in the area

Way. Copies of the latter can be inspected at public libraries or district council offices. In the event of difficulty please contact the Public Rights of Way Manager (listed elsewhere).

Linked, or running close, to the Medway Valley Walk are a number of other walks, as follows:

North Downs Way

The Medway Valley Walk links with the North Downs Way, one of twelve National Trails in Britain, which runs for 153 miles (244.8km) between Farnham in Surrey and Dover in Kent, with an alternative loop through Canterbury branching off at Boughton Aluph. The route mainly follows the ridge of the North Downs and there are fine panoramic views.

Publications

'North Downs Way - National Trail Guide' - Neil Curtis, Aurum Press, 25 Bedford Avenue, London WC1B 3AT

'North Downs Way - A Users' Guide', Kent County Council, Planning Department, Springfield, Maidstone, Kent ME14 2LX.

'North Downs Way Walks - Circular Walks', Kent County Council Planning Department, Springfield, Maidstone, Kent ME14 2LX.

Saxon Shore Way

The Saxon Shore Way, running for 163 miles (260.8 km) from Gravesend in Kent round the ancient coastline to Hastings in Sussex, offers the long-distance walker an unrivalled diversity of scenery from the wide expanses of marshland bordering the Thames and Medway estuaries to the White Cliffs of Dover. There are panoramic views over Romney Marsh from the escarpment that marks the ancient coastline between Folkestone and Rye, and from the sandstone cliffs of the High Weald at Hastings.

The route is also rich in historical sites and literary associations. Here the Romans invaded Britain and, later, built the 'Saxon Shore' forts to defend the island against a new wave of invaders. Here St Augustine landed to bring the Gospel to the Anglo-Saxon Kingdom which would later fall to the Normans who, in their turn erected great fortresses like Dover Castle to defend their conquests.

The shoreline is also of interest to the naturalist because of its importance as a feeding and roosting place for wintering and migratory birds.

The route is waymarked with a distinctive red horned helmet symbol.

Publication

'Saxon Shore Way' - Bea Cowan, Aurum Press, 25 Bedford Avenue, London WC1B 3AT

Wealdway

The Wealdway is an attractive scenic route running for 80 miles (128 km) across south-east England from the Thames estuary, over the North Downs and the Weald to the English Channel at Beachy Head. The route starts in Kent at the historic port of Gravesend and continues through Cobham with its Dickensian associations and over the dry valleys of the North Downs to the River Medway and Tonbridge.

The Wealdway is an interesting route with few major towns or settlements and gives many the opportunity to enjoy an unspoilt part of the South East. The route continues across the Weald and on through Ashdown Forest to Eastbourne at the foot of the South Downs.

Publications

'Wealdway' - Geoffrey King, Wealdway Steering Group, c/o 11 Old London Road, Brighton, East Sussex BN1 8XR

'Wealdway Accommodation Guide' - Wealdway Steering Group, as above.

'Guide to the Wealdway' - John Mason, Constable and Co, 11 Orange Street, London WC2H 3EW

'The Wealdway and the Vanguard Way' - Kev Reynolds, Cicerone Press, 2 Police Square, Milnthorpe, Cumbria

Greensand Way

The Greensand Way, as its name implies, follows the Greensand ridge across Surrey and Kent, between Haselmere and Hamstreet, and provides a long distance walking route of about 110 miles (176 km) across some of the most attractive countryside in south-east England.

The Kent section takes the route along the ridge by Chartwell, Toy's Hill, then through Sevenoaks Weald, Knole Park and on to West Peckham before leaving the Greensand ridge to cross the Medway flood plain at Yalding.

The route quickly ascends the ridge again and passes through the villages of

Linton, Sutton Valence, Ulcombe and Egerton through orchards and hop gardens, with many glorious views over the Weald to the south. The ridge becomes indistinct beyond Great Chart, but the route crosses an attractive, rolling landscape of farmland and woodland. The Greensand Way eventually joins the Saxon Shore Way at Hamstreet.

Publications

'Greensand Way in Kent' - Kent County Council, Planning Department, Springfield, Maidstone, Kent ME14 2LX

'Greensand Way in Surrey' Surrey County Council, Public Relations Unit, County Hall, Kingston upon Thames, Surrey. KT1 2DN

Eden Valley Walk

The Eden Valley Walk enables the walker to explore and experience the variety of countryside along the valleys of the River Eden and River Medway between Edenbridge and Tonbridge.

This 15-mile (24 km) linear recreation walking route passes through the High Weald Area of Outstanding Natural Beauty and is of interest for its natural history and archaeological, historical and architectural features. The route gives walkers the opportunity of enjoying a rolling landscape of ridges and valleys as its centre with a patchwork of small fields, hedges and broad-leaved woods.

Upstream the route traces the River Eden as it meanders through a flatter pastoral landscape. Historic houses set in parkland are passed en route, whilst downstream the route keeps company with the River Medway through Haysden Country Park.

Publication

'Eden Valley Walk' - Kent County Council, Planning Department, Springfield, Maidstone, Kent ME14 2LX

High Weald Walk

The High Weald Walk is a 27$^1/_2$-mile (44 km) circular route passing through an

Area of Outstanding Natural Beauty around Tunbridge Wells.

It gives walkers the opportunity of enjoying an undulating walk through the attractive countryside of the High Weald. It passes through the villages of Southborough, Pembury, Frant, Groombridge and Speldhurst.

The route is of interest for its natural history, archaeological, historical and architectural features. The Walk passes through a rolling landscape of ridges and valleys with a patchwork of small fields, hedges, broad-leaved woods and parkland.

Publication

'Along and Around the High Weald Walk' - Kent County Council, Planning Department, Springfield, Maidstone, Kent ME14 2LX

Further information and References

Bibliography

Buildings of England, West
Kent and The Weald (The)
John Newman
Penguin

Classic Walks in Southern
England
Kev Reynolds
Oxford Illustrated Press

Companion Guide to Kent
& Sussex (The)
Keith Spence
Collins

Exploring Kent Churches
John E Vigar
Meresborough Books

Friars, Aylesford (The)
Jarrold Colour Publications

Hops & Hop Picking
Richard Filmer
Shire Publications

Kent
Richard Church
Robert Hale

King's England: Kent (The)
Arthur Mee
Hodder & Stoughton

Portrait of the River
Medway
Roger Penn
Robert Hale

Rural Rides
William Cobbett

Shire County Guide: Kent
John E Vigar
Shire Publications

Visitor's Guide to Kent (The)
Kev Reynolds
Moorland Publishing

Walking in Kent
Kev Reynolds
Cicerone Press

Starkey's Castle Farm

Table of Historical Periods

Period	Range	Group
Mesolithic	10000 - 3500BC	*Prehistoric*
Neolithic	3500 - 2000BC	
Bronze Age	2000 - 800BC	
Iron Age	800 BC - AD 43	
Roman	43 - 410	
Anglo Saxon	410 - 1066	
Norman	1066 - 1154	
Plantagenet	1154 - 1399	*Medieval*
Lancastrian	1399 - 1461	
Yorkist	1461 - 1485	
Tudor	1485 - 1603	*Renaisance*
Elizabethan	1558 - 1603	
Stuart	1603 - 1714	
Jacobean	1603 - 1649	
Commonwealth	1649 - 1660	
Restoration	1660 - 1702	
Queen Anne	1702 - 1714	
Hanoverian	1714 - 1901	
Georgian	1714 - 1837	
Regency	1810 - 1820	
Victorian	1837 - 1901	
Edwardian	1901 - 1910	
Windsor	1910 - Present Day	

Table of Architectural Periods

Period	Range	Group
Romanesque	1066 - 1190	
Early English	1190 - 1280	*Gothic*
Decorated	1280 - 1380	
Perpendicular	1380 - 1550	
Classical	1550 - 1810	
Gothic & Classical Revivals	1810 - 1914	
Modern	1914 - Present Day	

Country Access Charter

Your rights of way are:
- Public footpaths - on foot only.
- Bridleways - on foot, horseback and pedal cycle.
- Byways - (usually old roads) most roads used as public paths and, of course, public roads - all traffic.

Use maps, signs and waymarks. Ordnance Survey Pathfinder and Landranger maps show most public rights of way.

On rights of way you can:
- Take a pram, pushchair or wheelchair if practicable.
- Take a dog (on a lead or under close control).
- Take a short route round an illegal obstruction or remove it sufficiently to get past.

You have a right to go for recreation to:
- Public parks and open spaces - on foot.
- Most commons near older towns and cities - on f and sometimes on horseback.
- Private land where th owner has a formal agreement with the l authority.

In addition you can use t following by local or established custom or con - ask for advice if you are unsure:
- Many areas of open country like moorland, fe and coastal areas, especially those of the National Trust, and mos commons.
- Some woods and forest especially those owned the Forestry Commissi
- Country parks and pic sites.
- Most beaches.
- Towpaths on canals and rivers.
- Some land that is being rested from agriculture, where notices allowing access are displayed.
- Some private paths and tracks.

sent sometimes extends
o riding horses and pedal
cles.

our information:
ounty and metropolitan
strict councils and
ondon boroughs have a
uty to protect, maintain
nd record rights of way,
nd hold registers of
commons and village
greens - report to them
any problems
encountered.

Obstructions, dangerous
animals, harassment and
misleading signs on rights
of way are illegal.

If a public path runs along
the edge of a field, it must
not be ploughed or
disturbed.

A public path across a
field can be ploughed or
disturbed to cultivate a
crop, but the surface must
be quickly restored and
the line of the path made
apparent on the ground.

Crops (other than grass)
must not be allowed to
inconvenience the use of a

right of way, or prevent
the line from being
apparent on the ground.

❖ Landowners can require
you to leave land to which
you have no right of
access.

❖ Motor vehicles are
normally permitted only
on roads, byways and
some roads used as public
paths.

❖ Follow any local byelaws.

And, wherever you go,
follow the Country Code:
❖ Enjoy the countryside and
respect its life and work.

❖ Guard against all risk of
fire.

❖ Fasten all gates.

❖ Keep your dogs under
close control.

❖ Keep to public paths
across farmland.

❖ Use gates and stiles to
negotiate fences, hedges
and walls.

❖ Leave livestock, crops and
machinery alone.

❖ Take your litter home.

❖ Help to keep all water
clean.

❖ Protect wildlife, plants and
trees.

❖ Take special care on
country roads.

❖ Make no unnecessary
noise.

This charter is for practical
guidance in England and
Wales only. Fuller advice is
given in a free booklet 'Out
in the Country' available
from Countryside
Commission Postal Sales, PO
Box 124, Walgrave,
Northampton NN6 9TL,
telephone (01604) 781848.
Published with kind
permission of the
Countryside Commission.

Apple blossom

Biographies

Sandra Fernandez

Born in Bombay, Sandra came to live in England in 1966. She attended the  Harrow College of Art, specialising in illustration, and the Royal College of Art, studying natural history illustration.

She has worked for the National Trust on their coast and country posters, and the book 'The National Trust Nature Companion'. She has also worked for the graphics department at London Zoo.

At present she works as a freelance illustrator from her home in Marden, Kent.

Kev Reynolds

For more than 17 years Kev Reynolds was the warden of Crockham Hill Youth Hostel in north-west Kent before becoming a freelance writer, photographer and lecturer specialising in countryside and mountain topics.

Author of hundreds of articles and over 20 books, his work takes him to some of the most dramatic corners of the world. But not even the mountains of the Himalayas can limit his love for the landscapes of Kent through which he has been happily wandering for the past 20-odd years.

Kev Reynolds is married and has two daughters.

Eila Lawton

Eila is a New Zealander whose love of the British countryside has helped to turn a fleeting visit to the United Kingdom into a stay of some twenty years.

She has been able to share that interest with many of in her work as Education Officer for Surrey Wildlife Trust and as a lecturer in countryside recreation at Merrist Wood College.

Eila is now working from h home in Surrey as a freelan countryside interpreter.